# GETTING TO VITO™

*the Very Important Top Officer*

10 Steps to VITO's Office

# ANTHONY PARINELLO

VITO | SELLING

WILEY

JOHN WILEY & SONS, INC.

Published by John Wiley & Sons, Inc. Hoboken, New Jersey.
Published simultaneously in Canada.

For general information on our other products and services please contact our Customer Care Department within the U.S. at (800) 762-2974, outside the United States at (317) 572-3993 or fax (317) 572-4002.

Wiley also publishes its books in a variety of electronic formats. Some content that appears in print may not be available in electronic books. For more information about Wiley products, visit our website at www.wiley.com.

*Library of Congress Cataloging-in-Publication Data:*

Parinello, Anthony.
  Getting to VITO (the very important top officer) : 10 steps to VITO's office / Anthony Parinello.
      p.   cm.
  ISBN 0-471-67519-9 (pbk.)
  1. Selling.   2. Sales personnel—Training of.   3. Chief executive officers.   I. Title.
HF5438.25.P3615 2005
658.85—dc22

                                                                      2004020267

Printed in the United States of America.
10 9 8 7 6 5 4 3 2 1

In Memory of
My brother Al:
The leader of the band

# VITO | SELLING

A personal message from Tony Parinello:

In 1995 I created a new lexicon for salespeople in America called *Selling to VITO, the Very Important Top Officer*. Times change, and so do the challenges we salespeople face.

The book you now hold in your hands is the flagship of an epic new series that will totally embody the spirit of VITO selling for the 21st century. From this point on, you will be offered best-practices education and coaching in every aspect of Very Important Top Officer selling imaginable, from prospecting to building unshakably loyal customers. This all-new series of VITO selling will provide you with online downloads, virtual seminars, and personal coaching, all tightly focused on one single goal: getting to the top and staying there.

Welcome to the new generation—welcome to VITO selling.

Visit www.vitoselling.com or call 800-777-VITO.

Have a stellar day!

*Tony*

Tony

# CONTENTS

# ACKNOWLEDGMENTS

I want to thank the following individuals for the both of us—you, the reader, and me, the author. If it wasn't for these silent soldiers we would never have met. A high-five to the entire team at John Wiley & Sons: They are a true pleasure to work with. Many thanks to Susan Dodson and the great team at Graphic Composition, Inc. for the layout and editing. Thanks to my customers for trusting me with their salespeople. Thanks to the alumni of my VITO live seminars for keeping me on my toes. A special thanks to my family for their endless supply of love and encouragement. Thank you Suzanne for all of your ideas, humor, attention, love, and support during all of the early mornings. And thanks to my loyal followers and to you, the reader of this book, since without you there would be no need to write.

Please accept my deepest gratitude.

# Preface

*March 2004*

As the speaker stepped on to the stage the audience of more than 1,000 stood and began to applaud. A standing ovation *before* a single word was spoken. I had only seen this happen once before, and that was in Fort Lauderdale in 1992. My brother Al and I watched as Og Mandino took the stage. As the audience stood and began their clapping my brother said to me: "Bro, that will be you someday." My brother always had a way of making me feel just a little bit bigger, a little bit brighter, and a little bit more successful than I knew I was. Og and my brother Al were always an inspiration for me. Time catches up, though; it always does. Og Mandino passed away a few years later, and so did my brother. I never forgot the lessons that both of them taught me . . . and the opportunities they continue to guide me to.

*Think big, act big, and big results will happen.*

Now, as I stepped up to the podium and looked out at the audience standing and clapping, I choked up. I could swear that I saw Og and Al in the audience! What a moment. What had I done to deserve such respect from this group of individuals? What moved this audience of more than 1,000 academics, business leaders, and sales professionals to honor me with a standing ovation before I said a single word? I was humbled.

I have spent my entire adult professional life perfecting a particular skill. I say *perfecting* because I have been constantly changing it. Like anything else in this universe, it's either growing or it's dying. I prefer to grow, and I know you do too. That's why you picked up this book. In the chapters that follow, you will be reading about tactics and methods that I have personally created. I haven't copied, shadowed, hacked, or taken one idea from any other source. What follows is original Tony. If you want to take what you read in the chapters of this book and put it to work in your sales career, you'll need to show a little faith, you'll need to trust me, and you'll need to forget all about the past. Here's why.

I have personally taught over 1,500,000 salespeople my VITO tactics. And it never ceases to amaze me how people will automatically predict their *future* on the basis of what happened in the *past*. The past is the wrong information to look at! In the past, you were a different person. You weren't as smart as you are today. You weren't as old as you are today. The circumstances around you were not the same as they are today. Yesterday is old, virtually irrelevant information! Today—and specifically what you decide to *believe* today—has a *much* greater impact on where you end up than anything that you might have experienced *before* today.

So how does that relate to getting to VITO *today?* Selling today in *this* economy requires new beliefs, new ideas, and new techniques. And that's exactly what you're going to find in this book. What worked yesterday or didn't work yesterday has nothing to do with it. I am going to give you real-world, thought-leading ideas that can revolutionize your selling power and your future in sales. You and I can predict your future success by deciding to believe that what you learn in this book *can* work. Then *you* must consciously believe it *will* work.

This book will help you formulate your new beliefs and give you the tactics to support your efforts to get to the top of your mountain, to stand at the peak of your own success. The only favor I ask of you is that once you're standing at the top you turn and reach out to someone and make them feel a little bit bigger, a little bit brighter, and a little bit more successful than they might be thinking that they are.

Thank you for your trust in me.

*A kind word from a fellow salesperson . . .*

WOW! Your tactics really work! I've been calling on a particular "Seemore" in a high value account for no less than F-I-V-E YEARS! Never has she responded to any of my previous 12 letters or umpteen voicemails.

So, I followed all of your steps for gathering critical VITO information, formulated the correspondence "wave" following your instructions to the "T." Then, at the appointed time I called and found out that VITO was on vacation so, then I left a voice mail message just like you said. Then, one week later I faxed a message just like you said. Then, the most unusual thing that's ever happened to me happened. VITO called *me* to set an appointment.

Pinch me, I must be dreaming.

I know you get stories like this all the time, but who doesn't like to get a pat on the back? I just wanted to say thank you, Tony.

Here's to OUR greater success,

Gary Bollinger-Smith
Seattle Wa.


*IMPORTANT NOTE:*
THE CONTENTS OF THIS BOOK COULD CHANGE YOUR LIFE.

# Don't Skip This Part

### THE CAST OF CHARACTERS

I thought about calling this part of the book the Introduction, but I figured that if I did that, you might not read it. That would be a problem, because this is the part of the book where you learn about all the key people in the great and rewarding drama that you're holding in your hands: *Getting to VITO.*

### MEET VITO

VITO is the Very Important Top Officer—the person with the ultimate veto power. VITO is the real "approver" of your sale.

This book will show you how to sell today and in the years to come. This book will be automatically updated as the selling environment changes. How? Not by just-in-time printing but by inviting you to go to a special Web site, www.gettingtovito.com, where you'll find current, up-to-date information for free, as well as additional materials available for a fee.

### LET'S GET FOCUSED

Getting to VITO focuses on the most important step of all in your sales work: getting to the person who has veto power over the decision to buy from you. Within this book, you will find powerful, proven tactics that really do result in getting to VITO. If you do what I say, you will increase the average size of your sale, and you'll make the sale in less time. There are many other benefits that will unfold in the chapters that follow. Take advantage of all of them.

### MEET SEEMORE

"Seemore" is the person in almost every account you want to sell your stuff to who always wants to *see more* of everything: you, meetings, presentations, demonstrations, site visits, lunches, donuts with little sprinkly things on top . . . you name it. Getting to VITO isn't about getting around Seemore or toasting Seemore to a crisp. Getting to VITO isn't about forgetting Seemore exists. Getting to VITO is all about putting VITO first in *all* of your attempts to sell . . . and putting Seemore second.

## MEET TOMMIE

"Tommie" is VITO's personal assistant. Tommie is closer to VITO than almost anyone at VITO Inc. Tommies are playing a more important role than ever before in corporate America. These trusted advisors really do know who's who . . . and who's doing what to whom. You'll do your sales career a big favor if you simply *treat Tommie like VITO.* You'll learn all about this too.

## AND THE MOST IMPORTANT PLAYER OF ALL . . .

Then, of course, there's you, the salesperson. You'll soon find out that there are plenty of tactics and new ideas for you to deploy. I want to let you know that you will not be the first to use what you will read about here. Over the past 15 years or so I've trained hundreds of thousands of salespeople to do what you're about to learn how to do. Some of the biggest companies in America pay me a lot of money to train their people how to do what I'm about to teach you. There's only one reason to do that: This system has been tested, and it works.

## AND THEN THERE'S ME . . .

I am totally passionate about and committed to the topic of VITO. I've focused on this topic in my books, in numerous articles, and in my audio programs and training seminars. What you're about to read is the culmination of all of these assets and the experience that I've gathered by personally approaching VITO and by learning from the experiences of my distinguished (and, yes, now wealthy) alumni.

My thought for you is that you should take what you are about to learn and *use it.*

Enjoy the journey!

*Tony*

Anthony Parinello

# Part One

---

# VITO SELLING: THE NEW GENERATION

# 1

---

# SETTING THE STAGE

**VITO Principle #1: Everything changes.**

Who is VITO?

VITO is the Very Important Top Officer—the man or woman who sits at the top of every single one of your target groups of prospects and customers who has the ultimate authority to make your sale materialize or disappear.

If VITO doesn't want to buy your stuff, the sale *is not* going to happen, no matter how many purchasing peons, interns, or technical experts say it's a great idea. Ever had a "sure thing" sale evaporate mysteriously? Five will get you ten that VITO, whom you never met, happened to mention to someone that what you were offering didn't seem like a great idea. Whoosh. You went from the hot new thing to radioactive in 10 seconds.

If VITO does want to buy your stuff, then the sale *is* going to happen, no matter how many senior VPs, entrenched suppliers, or relatives of the current vendor think it's a dumb idea to buy from you.

You want VITO on your side. This book is about *getting* VITO on your side.

. . .

I've spent a good many years writing articles and books, creating audio programs, building e-learning lessons, and teaching and coaching salespeople how to get appointments with VITO—the person who has the ultimate veto power. And over the years, like everything else in this universe, the process has changed.

Why? VITO has changed. Levels of authority continue to migrate upward within the enterprise. The tougher regulatory and legal environment of the last few years has made VITO more cautious. When people at the top exercise caution, they typically delegate and empower others in an effort to mitigate risk.

So I'll share with you, right now, the big lesson I've learned about VITO since I wrote my first book. It is this: Contrary to popular opinion (and my own assessment in the early 1990s), today's VITOs aren't really risk takers.

Actually, by the time VITO approves a decision—either through empowerment, delegation, or (gasp!) taking direction from individuals lower down and higher up in the executive ranks of VITO Inc.— the "risk" has typically become nonexistent. The decision turns into a well-informed strategic choice, one that puts *someone else's* neck on the line. (Or, better yet, a bunch of someone elses'.)

I realize that there are dangers in any generalization, and I know that what I've just described is not the way *all* VITOs operate these days. But it is an increasingly common pattern in today's business environment, and it seems likely to me—given some of the challenges faced by a number of visible "hard-charging" executives who really were serious risk takers—to remain a common pattern in years to come.

### DON'T KILL THE MESSENGER!

You're not going to like the facts of selling life that you're about to read. Just remember that I am on your side, and when you get to the end of this chapter I will still be on your side.

Ready? Here are six things you need to acknowledge about your selling career.

1. Right now, your sales cycle is, in all likelihood, about 50% longer than it can and should be.

2. You've been lied to repeatedly by the decision makers you've been dealing with for lo these many years. They've told you that they have the authority to say No to the vendors they deal with. They really don't have this power.
3. You've been selling to individuals who don't like to be sold to.
4. You've been annoying the hell out of them in the process.
5. Whether you realize it now or not, every VITO has a VITO.
6. If you want to sell to a VITO, you have to think like a VITO.

Let's look at each of these in depth.

## THING YOU NEED TO ACKNOWLEDGE ABOUT YOUR SELLING CAREER #1:

*Your Sales Cycle Is 50% Longer than It Should Be.*

I know, I know. The threadbare phrase "time is money" has been beaten into your skull for years. But is that any reason to ignore it?

The cost of a person-to-person "sales call" continues to rise in too many of today's sales organizations. Many sales managers still insist on getting salespeople to focus on "activity"—and not on results. In startling numbers, lines of business executives (like VPs of sales) are watching their ROS (return on sales) dwindle.

And guess what?

While all of this is happening, you and your contemporaries are, in all likelihood, using tactics that are actually lengthening rather than shortening your sales cycle! That means you're making these already lousy numbers *worse,* not better!

Dubious? Don't be. In the pages that follow, you'll learn what the (all-too-common) problems are and how to turn them around.

## THING YOU NEED TO ACKNOWLEDGE ABOUT YOUR SELLING CAREER #2:

*You've Been Lied to: Decision Makers Really Cannot Say No.*

There are, by my count, five important players in each and every account that you and I sell to. For now, I want to focus on the role of just one of these players: the Decision Maker, or DM.

### Fact Number One

The DMs' job is to say Yes. They have to. It's in their job description.

They have a need to fill, a job to do, and they need the help of "business partners" to do it. Keep in mind, then, that whenever you get what sounds like a No from a DM, *that means that they have said Yes to someone else,* like your competition. I know that's not cool, but that's the way it is.

### Fact Number Two

In the not-so-distant past (like, say, within the last 12 to 24 months) a few players changed their roles in your prospects' and customers' organization. You most likely didn't notice this, mainly because your prospects and customers didn't want you to know anything about it.

But it happened. DMs grew in numbers. They are now sprinkled all over the enterprise. And they tend to act out a role in our sales process that looks a lot more important than it really is.

DMs did at one time actually possess the "signature authority" for some pretty substantial numbers. Example: I sell to large Fortune 500 organizations. The VP of sales is typically the person who signs my agreement when I get a "yes" answer. In days past, the VP of sales had decision authority for upwards of $250,000. Today, that same VP in that same Fortune 500 account has a $2,500 authority level.

Look at it again. *Was:* a quarter of a million bucks. *Is:* twenty-five hundred bucks.

DMs are not about to tell us about this (very important!) trend. So, then, who is making the *real* decision?

Consider the following situation.

### Imaginary Case Study

Ms. VITO Importanta, the CEO of VITO, Inc., wants to capture the Pacific Rim opportunity for her line of wireless products. She's done her own research, and she's confident that her vision and mission will take the competition by surprise and win the market share that she needs to attract round two of investors. Her most trusted line-of-business executive, who has proven his ability to get things done ahead of time and under budget, is her chief operations officer (COO), Mr. Joe Kickass.

Mr. Kickass is empowered, during a simple one-on-one meeting with Ms. Importanta, to find all of the necessary channels to make this push across the Pacific Ocean a reality. The COO will take all of the *tactical* steps to make this happen. Ms. Importanta ends her directive with these words: "Kickass, once you've decided on the right suppliers, pass them by me *before* you sign anything."

What just took place? Ms. Importanta *kept* her veto power . . . and turned over the *risk* to Mr. K.

So here's what the situation looks like to the *typical* salesperson: Mr. K is the Decision Maker. The buck stops right on his desk. The typical salesperson thinks, "If Kickass says 'No,' I'm out of the game. If Kickass says 'Yes,' I just hit pay dirt."

*Wrong on both counts!*

If you think that the formal Decision Maker (Joe Kickass) is *the* person who is approving your sale, I have news for you. The numbers show different. The numbers also show that you're going to be surprised during your discussions with Mr. Kickass *after he says "yes"* to you, and most of the time you are not going to be pleasantly surprised.

A recent poll of my *Selling to VITO* alumni indicates that more often than not when a DM says "you're in the running and everything is looking good," *your sale is still very much in jeopardy.* A whopping 30% of the time the sale is denied. Even if you look at the world with that famous cup-half-full perspective, that means you're only getting seven out of ten deals, when you thought you had ten out of ten. Ouch!

### Who's Who Continues to Change

The business landscape has changed since I wrote *Selling to VITO*, and so have the players and their roles. Here's the lineup (from the bottom up) as it appears today, in the twenty-first century:

- Recommenders
- Influencers
- Decision Makers

- Approvers
- Board members

Note: In cases where you're selling to an enterprise that does not currently have any board members, not to worry . . . your job just got a little easier.

Empowerment in today's business world works like this:

Board members advise and empower Approvers to overaccomplish each and every one of their goals, plans, *and* objectives, especially year-end shareholder distributions.

Approvers empower Decision Makers by telling them to sign on the dotted line . . . *after* reporting to the Approver as to what their preferences are.

Decision Makers empower Influencers by telling them to make the selection and report to the DM as to what their preferences are. *But notice this:* Influencers invariably interpret, and advertise, this job of theirs as "making the decision," which is not the case.

Influencers empower Recommenders by asking them to be on a committee to make recommendations, which (as you probably already know) may or may not be considered, or even noticed, by the Influencer.

Recommenders empower nobody . . . *unless* they happen to occupy one of the other roles at the same time. It is a complex but unavoidable fact of business life in the twenty-first century that people sometimes play two, three, four, or all five of the roles outlined here at the same time!

Note: It's common in smaller organizations to have one individual playing multiple roles. Keep in mind that lower-level players don't normally play the role of a higher-placed individual, although they would have you think otherwise.

## THING YOU NEED TO ACKNOWLEDGE ABOUT YOUR SELLING CAREER #3:

*You've Been Selling to Individuals Who Don't Like to Be Sold To.*

Consider the case of a salesperson selling human resources (HR) outsourcing. She calls on the head of the HR department. Let's listen in on the call:

IMA GOGETTER, SALESPERSON: "Ms. Skepticala, our organization can reduce your department's direct cost and size by 75% while at the same time guaranteeing compliance with all of the state and federal regulations. Furthermore, our outsourcing team will manage and maintain your department's current workload without the unintentional inefficiencies you're currently experiencing."

MS. REELA SKEPTICALA, HEAD OF HUMAN RESOURCES: "Hmmm. Send me some information and I'll get back to you."

If Ms. Skepticala embraces this "solution," she will be out of a job! Skip this kind of exchange. Follow these three simple rules.

Rule Number One: *Don't waste your time trying to sell to anyone who makes less money than you do.*

Rule Number Two: *Never ask anyone who makes less money than you do to sell for you.*

Rule Number Three: *Make your first call to the same titles your own CEO would call.*

## THING YOU NEED TO ACKNOWLEDGE ABOUT YOUR SELLING CAREER #4:

*You've Been Annoying the Hell Out of the People You've Been Trying to Sell To.*

If you violate rules one and two, previously outlined, you won't just be wasting your own time. You will be building *enemies* within the organization you are trying to sell to.

Don't do it.

## THING YOU NEED TO ACKNOWLEDGE ABOUT YOUR SELLING CAREER #5:

*Every VITO Has a VITO.*

I am going to get into this topic in much greater depth in the pages that follow, but let me make the point here briefly to underline its importance. Every VITO has a VITO.

VITOs take direction from those individuals who are higher up in the "food chain". While I was writing my *Wall Street Journal* best-selling book *Think and Sell Like a CEO* I interviewed over one hundred VITOs. To prepare for this daunting task and to make editing the material as manageable as possible, I created a form with 15 different questions that I would be asking each CEO, president, and owner that I would be interviewing. Everyone that I interviewed had different answers to each question . . . with the exception of two questions. Both of these questions were answered in exactly the same way by each VITO I interviewed.

The first question was:

*Who has the power to interrupt you from your busy day and stop whatever you're doing so that you take their call?*

Here's the answer that *always* came back:

*One of my board members.*

Food for thought, yes?
Now, let's look at the second question.

## THING YOU NEED TO ACKNOWLEDGE ABOUT YOUR SELLING CAREER #6:

*If You Want to Sell to VITO, You Have to Think Like VITO.*

Here's the second question that was answered in precisely the same way by every one of the more than 100 VITOs I interviewed:

*What's the single most important aspect of your operation that is critical to your overall success?*

Here's the answer that *always* came back:

*Following a plan and a process*

I discovered that the most successful VITOS made sure their companies had processes for *everything!* Finance, manufacturing, marketing, customer service, and yes, even sales. If it mattered to the organization, the most successful top bananas had figured out a way to turn it into a process. Interesting, yes?

A process, of course, is basically a recipe. It's the proven "what to do" and the reliable "when to do it" of what VITO (or you) plans to carry out. It's the ingredients and the sequence used to create any desired result (like increasing shareholder value or making a sale).

So here's what you have to understand. The most successful VITOs start with the end in mind, then look for a process that will deliver that goal. They begin by stating what they want as a positive picture for their mind's eye. For instance:

*My goal is to capture the Pacific Rim market for my wireless products.*

Not:

*I don't want to lose market share to my competitors.*

If you stop and think about it, it makes sense for us to state our desired end result in a positive way. This is because the human mind (that includes you, me, and VITO) focuses powerfully on whatever we give it, *even when what we focus on contradicts the logical sense of what we think we are asking our mind to do.* So, for example, if we tell our mind, "I don't want to lose market share to my competition," guess what outcome our brains are most likely to fixate on? *Losing market share!* That's what will come back to us. If, on the other hand, we say to ourselves, "*My goal is to capture the Pacific market for my wireless products,*" our mind fixates on the *desired* outcome: *capturing the Pacific market.* Phrasing commands and questions in a positive manner is extremely important in running a company, making sales . . . and, indeed, in just about every aspect of life you can imagine.

Here's the payoff: I learned to my astonishment that the vast majority of successful VITOs I was interviewing made a habit of *seeing* themselves being successful. They habitually *visualized* positive outcomes, as I've described . . . and, as a result, they were much more likely to attain them.

You can understand, then, why I'm going to insist that you *see* yourself taking each of the ten steps to VITO's office that I'll be explaining to you throughout the remaining chapters of this book. This visualization is a very important part of the sales success that awaits!

Here's an example of a *positive* message for you to use before turning to Chapter 2:

*"I see myself making more sales with VITOs than ever before. I see myself realizing larger than average initial sales in a shorter amount of time, and getting all of the add-on business and referrals that I've worked hard for and deserve from my existing customers."*

Let's push on to the next chapter!

# 2

# RESULTS AND THE PROCESS THAT DRIVES THEM

> **VITO Principle #2: A well-defined process will always yield a well-desired result.**

Now that you've completed Chapter 1, you know that our selling environment isn't what it used to be. You know that what's worked in the past will not work today. So it's not going to come as a huge surprise to you that I'm going to ask you to take a long, hard look at your sales process—and get really honest with yourself as to what's working and what's not.

Please fill in the blanks in the following form.

How long does it take you to sell whatever it is you're selling?
_____

How many tasks (or, if you prefer, steps) does your sales process have? _____

List each task and step separately. Identify the average number of hours, days, weeks, or months it takes to perform each step:

| Task | Step Number | Time |
|---|---|---|
| _____ | _____ | _____ |
| _____ | _____ | _____ |
| _____ | _____ | _____ |
| _____ | _____ | _____ |
| _____ | _____ | _____ |
| _____ | _____ | _____ |
| _____ | _____ | _____ |
| _____ | _____ | _____ |
| _____ | _____ | _____ |
| _____ | _____ | _____ |
| _____ | _____ | _____ |
| _____ | _____ | _____ |

Total: _____ _____

NOTE: The reason that there are only 12 lines above is that it's been my personal experience that if a sales process has more than 12 steps it's just too darned long. At that point, it's not selling, but some form of engineering!

## LET'S GET REALLY HONEST

Look closely at what you've just created. Take a few minutes to mull over it. If you skipped filling out the form, drop and give me 20 pushups or crunches in penance. *Fill out the form . . .* and then ask yourself the following questions:

1. "How many of these steps are a total waste of time for me?" Identify the culprits right now, while you're still focused on them. Then draw a line through those items and make a solemn vow not to invest any more of your time in them. Subtract that amount of time from your total.

2. "If I could change the way I sell (for example, by consistently gaining access to the Approver of the sale, i.e., VITO) what steps could I compress?" Now recalculate and subtract that amount of time from your total.

3. "If I could guarantee that the prospects that I approach would be predisposed to buy from me, what steps could I compress and or eliminate?" Yes, it's possible. You just don't know how yet, but once you figure out how to do this (we'll get to that in a minute), you won't want to connect with anyone *but* people who are predisposed to buy from you. Here again, recalculate and subtract that amount of time from your total.

4. "If I could totally rewrite my sales 'playbook,' what steps could I compress and/or eliminate?" Now recalculate and/or draw a line through the item(s) and subtract that amount of time from your total.

5. "Does my sales process follow the process that my prospect uses to buy?" Big question! We'll cover the implications of this important consideration in depth a little later on in the book. For now, just answer the question honestly for yourself. Yes or no?

What does your sales process total look like now? It should be at least 50% shorter.

Here's what I usually hear when I ask salespeople to complete this exercise: "Tony, I'm just a salesperson . . . get real! I can't change this stuff!"

Yada yada yada, that's the way we've always done it. Yada yada yada, "I can't get my manager to make any changes." Yada yada yada, "that's the way she wants it done." Yada yada yada, "I can't do anything about this." Yada yada yada, "I'm just a salesperson." Yada yada yada, "I don't write the rules, I just follow them."

Here, you try it. Fill in the blank below with your favorite phrase.

"Yada yada yada, I can't _____!"

Do yourself a very big favor and do it right now. Drop the apostrophe and "t" from the word *can't* and here's what you have:

I CAN!

Doesn't that feel better? This new outlook will serve your sales career much better than the old yada-yada-yada-I-can't-possibly-(whatever) model. It will help you when it comes to taking action on what you'll be learning in the pages that follow.

### FACTS TO CONSIDER

Fact #1: Eighty-five percent of CEOs, presidents, and owners of companies were once salespeople, and the other 15% really know the importance of sales and the people who make them happen (hey, that's you!). If necessary, walk into your sales manager's (or VITO's) office and say, right out loud, "You know what? In order to compress my sales cycle and deliver more revenue for this company, I want to try something new. Here's what I have in mind . . ."

Watch the grin that spreads over your boss's face.

*Translation:* If you want anything to change in your sales process, take your cause up with your higher-ups!

Fact #2: Nothing happens until something is sold.

*Translation:* Your voice is important, and your position is critical to the success of the company you work for. The truth is that you're a critical player. So act like one.

Fact #3: Salespeople generate the lifeblood of the company . . . which would be REVENUE.

*Translation:* There is no other job that is as pivotal and critical to the overall success of the company you work for than your job. Without the revenue that you're creating, *the lights would go out.*

Fact #4: Revenue-generating activities have the greatest impact on shareholder value.

*Translation:* Shareholder value and its growth are the single most important responsibilities of your own VITO. Here again, if you've got an idea about how to increase ROS (return on sales), take it to the top.

Fact #5: You have the power to change anything in your sales process that will make the sale happen faster. (Just try it. See if anyone files a complaint.)

*Translation:* Stop whining! Start selling large and living large! Don't make me say this again! Or you'll have to drop and give me another 20!

## CHALLENGING UNHEALTHY BELIEFS

I'd like to challenge you right now to consider the possibility that some of the beliefs that you are currently using in your sales work are not healthy. I'll bet you a nickel that some of your current beliefs do not serve you and do not contribute to your overall success in sales.

Here's an example of the kind of belief I'm talking about: "I have to follow my own sales process to make the sale."

Most salespeople believe this. Yet experience has shown me time and time again that the best way to influence the outcome of any sale is to understand *how your prospect's organization goes about the process of purchasing products, services, and solutions*—and then tailor your sales process to match your prospect's buying process.

## LOOK AT HOW THEY SELL

Organizations and the individuals who run them—VITOs—are likely to take the same approach to buying that they do to selling. If the prospect that you want to sell to is in an environment that is governed by strict industry regulations and government stipulations, then your job is to make darned sure that your sales process and approach are tight as a drum! Everything should have a backup; everything should have a contingency plan; everything should add up, even if you compute the columns sideways.

Here's an example of what I mean. Suppose you're selling an accounting software package to the pharmaceutical industry, which happens to be one of the most tightly regulated industries in the free world. And suppose your "generic" marketing brochures and product information are vague and some what "slick."

Not good. Don't send 'em.

In fact, don't send anything to this group of target prospects that isn't 1000% verified in four dimensions. Make sure it's direct, to the point, and utterly accurate. And, last but not least, make sure it has absolutely no typos in it!

## LOOK AT THE SOCIAL PROOF

Does your target prospect use testimonials from existing customers to sing their praises? Or do they "blow their own horn"?

The answers to these questions will tell you whether your prospect organization has a tendency toward being "internally" or "externally" focused. In other words, if they liberally use customer testimonials in their marketing approach, they will be more open to understanding what *your* customers have to say. The opposite is also true.

Look at their advertising, their web site, their brochures, and whatever else you can track down. If one of the first elements you see is the logos of their customers, and/or accolades the company has received from industry experts, you can safely assume that this prospect will care about, and be eager to hear about, what *your customers* have to say. Use this knowledge to your best advantage!

## FIND OUT WHERE THEY ARE

Who is their current source of supply? When did they last purchase whatever it is you happen to be selling? What you're looking for is a pattern. Let's say for a moment that you're selling file management services to hospitals and law firms. You find out that a large hospital in your territory is looking to outsource its physical file storage and retrieval systems. On your first appointment, you discover that this hospital is using a system that was antiquated when it was first installed . . . five years ago!

What to do? Mirror and match. Your initial approach to this prospect should start by establishing where your product, service, and/or solution was *at the time they installed their system*. For example:

> YOU: "Five years ago, our storage and retrieval systems were (A, B, C), and today they are better because (D, E, F)."

What you *don't* want to do is open the discussion by saying, "Where the heck have you been for the past five years . . . under a rock?" The person you happen to be talking to may have made the decision to purchase whatever it is they are using today!

## FIND OUT ABOUT THEIR SALES FORCE

If your prospect organization has an indirect sales force, that fact will give you some indication as to their sensitivity to the all-important metric of ROS. Now, you may ask: What's their sensitivity got to do with your sales approach? Everything! If your approach is not cost and time efficient, their spoken (or, worse yet, unspoken) objection may just kill your sale!

Let's face it. A higher than necessary cost of sales eventually has to be paid for by the customer (with a higher purchase price) or by the selling organization's shareholders (with a lower than necessary shareholder value). In either case, VITO will not take your insensitivity to ROS kindly.

Play it safe. Trim the fat out of all of your pre-sales activities. Forget the fancy brochures, the expensive lunches, the sky-box tickets at the ball game, the ridiculous green fees, the freebees, the premature demos and presentations, the factory tours, and everything else. Make sure all of your pre-sales activities demonstrate that you have a mindful eye on your direct and indirect cost of sales.

## FIND OUT ABOUT THEIR REPUTATION IN THE MARKETPLACE

That's right. Forget about yourself and your organization for a moment, and picture your target prospect wearing a designer T-shirt that says, "It's all about me." For starters, try to find out:

- Their customer satisfaction ratings
- How many customers they have
- What industries they serve
- Who their competition is and how they stack up
- Who their customers are in your sales territory and if you can visit and/or talk to them

In all of your pre-sales efforts, you must strive to understand and respect your prospect's position in the marketplace. Make an effort to let VITO know that you will always look for ways to enhance that position. More on this later . . .

## FIND OUT ABOUT THEIR PRICE POSITION

If you know that the prospect you're targeting is positioned in their marketplace as the "high-price, high-quality" provider, and you happen to be selling the lowest price in town, you may have a problem on your hands!

If you possibly can, pick some other prospect to sell to. I can't begin to calculate how much of my precious selling time I've wasted over the years by not adhering to this simple truth and basically ignoring the fact that the price-quality and value ratios didn't match those of my prospects.

## FIND OUT HOW THEY SELL THEIR STUFF

If the VITO you want to get to uses the Internet to approach their prospects and sell their own stuff, you might want to try using similar approaches when getting to VITO. Over the years I've seen many, many sales go down in flames because they ignored this simple, powerful piece of advice.

Update everything! Make sure you can shift gears at a moment's notice. Be ready to use both traditional and cutting-edge communication and presentation strategies.

## FOUR STEPS TO AN EXTREMELY EFFECTIVE SALES PROCESS

Over the years I've interviewed, sold to, and built up some great working relationships with the VITOs of the world. As I've already mentioned, the most successful ones have created and follow a process for everything. Once it is in place, they embrace a four-step system to broadcast that process throughout their enterprise.

### *Step One: Analyze the Process*

VITOs delight in figuring out what's necessary . . . and figuring out what's excess baggage. Do you? In the chapters that follow I'll be challenging you to continually look at specific things you're currently doing in your sales process . . . and challenging you to shed what isn't working and replace it with something new. Are you willing to take the steps necessary to create change? Are you willing to take a bit of a risk? Good, I thought so.

### Step Two: Improve the Process

VITOs are on a constant "improvement patrol." You should be too. We have to look for ideas that will take whatever we're using and make it better. We can't be satisfied with what we're doing right now.

I invite you to use the ideas you will encounter in this book and measure their impact as accurately as possible. Then make small changes to improve your results. Always *measure what happened as a result of the changes you made.*

### Step Three: Control the Process

VITOs are control freaks. They see their world as consisting of elements they *can and do control.* Is that a "correct" way of looking at the world? That doesn't really matter. What matters is whether it's a *useful* way of looking at the world.

Whenever a potential sale disappoints you (the size of the sale was too small, the sale took too long, the sale didn't happen at all, whatever), *assume that the disappointment can be remedied next time around by changing something you control or influence.* Ask yourself questions like "What, if anything, did my plan and approach overlook?" "What did I overlook in my plan and approach?" *Do not* ask yourself disempowering questions like "Why do these things always happen to me?" or think "The competition sure is getting tough!"

### Step Four: Replicate the Process

It's cookie-cutting time! Once you've latched on to something that delivers the results you want, plug it in again next time around!

Before we continue and dive head first into Chapter 3, let's take a deep breath. Now, with plenty of oxygen rushing to our brains, let me ask you: What did you uncover as extra and unnecessary steps in your current sales process? Are you willing to use the four VITO proven steps to create a positive change in your sales work?

I thought so. Let's push on!

# 3

---

# VALUE VERSUS VALUES

VITOs live and breathe value.

If you don't "get" the concept of value, you'll miss out on sales heaven entirely and spend way too much time in sales hell.

In the old days, value was easy to understand. Basically, there were two types: hard and soft. However, today we must get our heads around no less than *seven* expressions of value.

Intrigued? Let's take a closer look.

## SOME DEFINITIONS

Let's define three different categories that our opportunities could possibly fit into:

- *VITO Suspects:* These are VITOs and/or the organizations they lead who have a need for your products, services, and/or solutions, but who have not yet had any direct contact with you or your organization.
- *VITO Prospects:* These are VITOs and/or the organizations they lead whom you have contacted, or who have contacted you, *and* who also have a need in one or more of the categories of value and values that are defined in this chapter.

- *VITO Customers:* VITOs and/or the organizations they lead who are *currently* buying from you. The operative word here is *currently.* If they are not currently buying from you, by default they will immediately fall into the category of "prospect."

## BACK TO THE FUTURE

There is no question in my mind that no matter what category—suspect, prospect, or customer—articulating relevant value to VITO is the key to opening up, marinating, and growing the business relationship. Following are the various areas of value that you and I and every other VITO salesperson must have an intimate and working knowledge of.

### Value Parameter #1: Hard-Dollar Value

This kind of value is tangible. It's easy to see and easy to measure. It's usually expressed in numbers and/or percentages. For example:

- a $53,000 increase in revenues
- a 14% decrease in time-to-market
- a $450,000 decrease in fixed expenses
- a 9% increase in production line efficiencies
- a 2% increase in shareholder value

What kind of hard-dollar results have *you* delivered to your current base of customers? If you don't know the answer to that question, you're not alone. Most of the salespeople I know don't really have a good grip on this topic either. That's why at the end of this chapter you'll be directed to the Internet to participate in a "Value Inventory" exercise that will help you get the answer. For now, just understand that hard-dollar value is *extremely* important to VITOs and that you're going to have to be able to identify it and quantify it.

### Value Parameter #2: Soft-Dollar Value

This kind of value is intangible. It's more difficult to see than hard-dollar value and is expressed using descriptive words or phrases. For example:

- reduced risk
- greater peace of mind
- greater focus on core competencies
- greater customer satisfaction
- increased brand awareness in the marketplace

What's important here is that you know what soft-dollar value you are delivering or have the potential of delivering to VITO. Here again, the e-lesson that you'll be completing at the end of this chapter will help you establish exactly what your value is.

IMPORTANT GETTING-TO-VITO CONCEPT:

VITOs are not going to waste their precious time picking apart *what* you sell . . . but they will take plenty of time to engage with the *results* your stuff has the potential of delivering, especially when those results are articulated in terms of hard- and/or soft-dollar value. Don't worry about product names, model numbers, or what you think your product *is*. Focus on the results.

### *Value Parameter #3: Value Harmony with Your Prospects*

The idea here is to single out particular suspects and prospects to approach based on your ability to match their value requirements in key areas. What's the sense of wasting our time with prospects that are not predisposed to buy from us?

Take the time and ask your very best customers the following questions. Once you are armed with the answers, you'll have an intuitive sense of which outfits match up with your company and which don't.

(By the way, if you personally don't have any customers yet, do this simple exercise: Ask your sales manager to take the ball and get these questions answered from some other sales rep's accounts. The more customers you ask these questions of, the more accurate your value profile will be.)

Ask your customers these questions:

1. What goals, plans, and/or objectives do you feel my organization has assisted your (department, division, organization) with?

2. What areas of your organization have experienced a positive result from the use of my products, services, and solutions?

3. What individuals within your organization have received the greatest benefit from the use of my products, services, and solutions?

Remember—the more people you ask these questions, the better your own value profile will be. Now, match this result with each new prospect you encounter. To do this you'll find some handy forms by going to this chapter's online assets: www.gettingtovito.com

### *Value Parameter #4: Value Targeting*

Once you have successfully obtained the answers to the questions listed, write in the title(s) of the individual(s) who answered the questions. Then, next to the person's title, insert the specific industries that your best customers reside in.

Now take a look at the patterns that emerge. What do you think would happen if you took the time to preselect potential suspects and prospects with *similar or identical* titles in *similar or identical* industries in your territory? How about bigger deals in less time!

In fact . . .

What do you think would happen if you chose *only* to engage in a sales cycle with people and organizations who matched the profile you just identified?

### *Value Parameter #5: Mutual Value*

Healthy business relationships, like healthy personal relationships, are two-way streets. So the question naturally becomes: "What value do your best customers deliver to you?" For example:

- Do they help you design new products?
- Do they provide testimonials?
- Do they willingly give you referrals?
- Do they give you all of the high-margin, add-on business you've worked hard for and deserve?
- Do they give you access up and down the hierarchy of their enterprise?
- Do they call you first when a need arises?

If you're shaking your head sideways in the No direction for any or all of these questions, guess what? You've got no mutual value, and that's not a good thing.

Initiating mutual value is *your job*. That's right. *You* need to take the lead on setting expectations with your very best customers. *You* need to share with *them* what *you* expect from the relationship!

### Value Parameter #6: Minimum Acceptable Value

We need to understand what's acceptable return on investment (and what's not acceptable return on investment) . . . from VITO's point of view. The key words here are *VITO's point of view.* It's difficult to establish this without first getting to VITO so you can ask the following questions. This may well be a small deviation from my earlier statement of contacting only organizations that are predisposed to buy from you, but it's well worth the trouble to find out.

I strongly suggest that, when the opportunity arises, you ask VITO right up front what type of return on investment (ROI) he or she needs to realize. Typically, you can find out what the VITO's acceptable ROI is by asking two kinds of questions:

- Goal-centric questions: "What payback amount (or percentage) over what period of time do you expect from being able to overachieve your _____?" (Fill in the blank with one of this VITO's goals, plans, or objectives.)
- Product-centric questions: "What payback amount (or percentage) over what period of time do you expect from investing in _____?" (Fill in the blank with your product category; e.g., supply chain management.)

If you *don't* have a track record of performance that proves you can easily measure up to VITO's expectation of ROI (see Value Parameter #3), I invite you to bail out of the opportunity, cut your losses, and move on to the next VITO.

I know that sounds scary, but it's been my experience that if I couldn't plausibly make the case that I could deliver the ROI "goods," then eventually the deal simply fell apart. No matter how hard I tried to make the shoe fit, it never did.

Save your time.

### *Value Parameter #7: Unique Value*

Have you ever been told by anyone that your product, service, or so-lution was a "commodity"? Have you ever wondered whether your stuff was being "commoditized" by the marketplace or the competi-tion?

Well, I believe that nothing that can affect a company's results is a commodity. Consider this, the word *commodity* is really a combina-tion of two words: *Commode,* which of course means "to dispel," and *oddity,* which of course means rarity. Thus, *commodity* means "to dispel rareness." I thought it was interesting and somewhat funny too!

Consider the following true story. Notice first that I was selling computer systems here—not degreasing components (thank good-ness).

Let's establish first that a salesperson who sells the cleaning sup-plies and the degreaser that's used to keep the production floor clean and safe would not normally take the time to approach the VITO of the prospect organization. That salesperson will sell at a much lower level, right? Because it's so obviously a commodity purchase. Why on earth would a VITO take the time to get involved in purchasing such a "commodity"? That's really the job of the senior buyer—wouldn't you agree?

Okay, here's what happened.

This was the largest production run in the history of the company. This contract award was given on two important criteria: cost and delivery.

The VP of operations noticed one of the facilities maintenance personnel cleaning up a high-grade oil spill in the forklift traffic lane. "Morning, Jake, how's it going?" The maintenance guy didn't even look up to see who was asking when he replied, "Trying like hell to get this mess cleaned up." The VP didn't even look back as he said, "I am sure you'll get it."

Two hours later, the first completed jet engine was being trans-ported to the flatbed tractor-trailer for delivery a full week ahead of schedule. The CEO had just called the customer to inform them of their accomplishment when line two lit up on the CEO's phone. After completing the brief call of congrats with his now very happy and impressed customer, Mickey picked up line two. The news came fast and hard. I could hear the excited voice of the VP of operations: "We just had an accident, no one's been hurt, but engine number one just fell off the transport! It wasn't the operator's fault . . . the lift skidded on something. We're checking everything out, but there's no way we'll meet the deadline of next week. We've got to start production from scratch."

I saw the anger well up inside the CEO's body. He jumped up from his chair and without a word left his office. I would later come to find out that an oil spill had been cleaned with an off-the-shelf cleaner, not the specified commercial cleaner that was supposed to be used. That stuff was out of stock. The residue that was left on the floor caused the accident.

The buyer whose job it was to make sure inventory was properly sustained was fired.

Jake, the maintenance guy, was put on probation.

I was given the sales order for the computer system that I was pitching the CEO in half the time that it would have taken me to get the order. Why? Because after witnessing that blunder I reconfigured my software, offering to include an "insurance" policy!

Oh, I wasn't selling insurance. All I did was include an inventory management system so VITO would never jeopardize another delivery and would never again be failed in the way his inventory system had failed him this time.

That add-on with hardware and software added another $150,000 to my sale. All because a "commodity"—the degreaser—wasn't available when it was needed the most. (In subsequent sales calls to other VITOs in the manufacturing industry, I shifted my approach from attempting to get VITO's attention using an "inventory control" pitch to one that addressed the need for safety and compliance.)

Whenever you are tempted to think that you sell a commodity, think again. Ask yourself: What unique value can I deliver?

Ask yourself:

- What happens if my customers can't get their hands on my product, service, or solution when they most need it?

- What's the most horrid event that could happen if my customers can't get my stuff to work?
- What's the ultimate consequence they will pay?

Before you push on to the next chapter, you may want to go on line to www.gettingtovito.com and download this chapter's for-free and for-fee online assets.

# 4

---

# YOUR PERSONAL VALUE

This topic and exercise are so important I've devoted an entire chapter to them. Do yourself a favor: Don't skip what follows!

Get a big piece of paper. Write your *entire* name on the top of the form (no initials allowed). If you're married and female, please go the extra distance and add your maiden name.

When you've done that, come back to this book and proceed with the instructions that follow, being sure not to leave any of the steps out.

Now you're going to create a "value acronym" for your own name.

For each letter in your name, select a word that you feel accurately describes your positive values, qualities, personality traits, and habits—at least on a good day!

*Rule number one:* You aren't your stuff! Stay away from words that would describe a favorite hobby, your career, or any material possessions.

*Rule number two:* Do this on your own. Don't use words that *other* people say represent you; use your own words.

*Rule number three:* Take your time with this exercise. If you get stuck, you can use a dictionary or thesaurus . . . but only as a last resort.

Take a look at my name.

A N T H O N Y F R A N K P A R I N E L L O

Here's how my initials create my acronym.

| VALUES and BELIEFS | QUALITIES and TRAITS |
|---|---|
| Trustworthy | Aggressive |
| Honest | Nurturing |
| Forthright | Overgenerous |
| Loyal | Reliable |
| Esteemed | Nimble |
| Affectionate | Yes (I live by the word "yes") |
| Noble | Nonconforming |
| Purposeful | Reckless |
| Altruistic | Knowledgeable |
| | Intuitive |
| | Lighthearted |
| | Optimistic |

That's me. And here's the point: Once I settle on the words . . . it's up to me to put *me* into my daily sales work.

## A WORD ABOUT VALUES

Values are our core operating principles. If we compromise or deviate in the smallest way from these basic values, the result is some type of short- or long-term negative consequences —perhaps even severe consequences! (I categorize the pain and loss of self-respect associated with subverting my own values as severe consequences.)

## A WORD ABOUT QUALITIES AND TRAITS

We may not *always* display these positive qualities and traits under *every* circumstance. Qualities and traits can tolerate change. For instance, being patient (not a trait of mine) can be considered a quality or trait, rather than a value. Let's say it's part of your acronym. Let's also say, though, that you've been waiting at the box office for a friend for the past 20 minutes and that the show started 10 minutes ago! When your friend finally shows up a full 45 minutes late with a lame excuse like "I couldn't find a parking space," no one in my circle of friends would blame you for being slightly (or even more than slightly) peeved, even if you usually *are* patient and consider that a strong suit.

## DO IT!

This exercise takes time and patience—and a good deal of scribbling and erasing. Once you're done with your first draft on that big piece of paper, you may want to transfer the results to this form:

Your name: _____

___  _____     ___  _____
___  _____     ___  _____
___  _____     ___  _____
___  _____     ___  _____
___  _____     ___  _____
___  _____     ___  _____
___  _____     ___  _____
___  _____     ___  _____
___  _____     ___  _____
___  _____     ___  _____

## A PROFOUND EXERCISE AND A PROFOUND QUESTION

If you do the exercise right, *your best self* is what shows up in the acronym.

The question now becomes . . . how do you *show* your true and best self to VITO—so you can become the competitive weapon of choice?

In my case, I ask this: Do I consistently show *my* unique and best value? Specifically, am I *really* purposeful in my sales approach? Am I trustworthy and honest at *all* times? Do I do as I say I will? Do I actually *show* my intuitive ways, and am I knowledgeable in a way that's meaningful?

Here's the bottom line: If you fall short of living up to and demonstrating your unique value in getting to VITO, you will lose your strongest competitive advantage . . . you! Once you identify those words and link them strongly to your own name, you will know what you have to live up to . . . and why!

And here, by the way, is the ultimate motivator. You'll know that if you *don't* demonstrate and live up to those values, then you may rest assured that you'll fail what I call . . .

## VITO'S FOUR-PART VALUE JUSTIFICATION TEST

If you've been in sales long enough to make even one sale, you already know that your prospect will at some point in time . . . after you pitch your stuff but *before* they actually buy your stuff . . . do what's known as a *justification*.

This is an indisputable law of sales. If you apply this law to VITO's world, you come up with the a four-part equation of justification that you *must* be ready to pass with all the confidence and commitment and positive value traits you can muster. (By the way, I learned these three simple yet profound ways of looking at justification from interviews and correspondence with over 100 CEOs, presidents, and owners of organizations.)

For VITO, justification inevitably boils down to a simple four-part risk/value equation. Taking only intelligent risks and cashing in on all the value is VITO's dream come true.

Check out this breakdown . . . then consider posting it where you can see it every day.

---

ITEM ONE: FINANCIAL JUSIFICATION, VITO STYLE
*Financial risk versus value*
VITOs ask themselves:
1. How much capital will this cost?
2. Whose money will be at risk?
3. What other financial and nonfinancial resources could this risk possibly affect?

---

### *Now Ask Yourself . . .*

How are you going to make your financial case? What dollar value do you personally, and as a representative of your organization, bring to the table? How does it make VITO's dollar risk more attractive? What, exactly, do you know about that risk? Specifically, what expenses and resources will VITO have to risk to take advantage of your product, service, or solution? What else needs to be purchased, built, modified, added, or whatever-ed in order for VITO to install and use whatever you're selling?

Here's an example. When I sold computer systems back in the late seventies, they required "data centers" to house them. These were special facilities that had raised floors, special power, and 24-hour air conditioning. (Yeah, yeah, I know. I'm dating myself.)

The point is, sometimes the expense for the facility was 50% of the cost of the equipment I was selling! And as if that weren't enough to fire-hose the deal, the computers had to be programmed by a staff of trained personnel.

Here's what I want you to come away with about financial risk. When making the sale to VITO *I had a responsibility to understand and articulate this risk* so my value analysis would completely—and confidently—offset the entire cost of my offering.

Next, let's look at how VITO looks at time and value.

Check out this breakdown . . . then consider posting it where you can see it every day.

---

ITEM TWO: TIME JUSTIFICATION, VITO STYLE

*Time-to-Value*

VITOs ask themselves:
1. How long will it take to realize the promised value?
2. What's being compromised during this time?
3. Are there gaps in the time-to-value timeline?
4. What will these time gaps cost?

---

### *Now Ask Yourself . . .*

In the not so perfect world of implementation plans, how long will it take VITO to realize *all* of the value of your offering? In other words, how can you use your personal value to answer the question "When is this stuff going to pay off?"

It's incredibly important for you and your organization to be conservative with your estimates of time-to-value. Your future in the marketplace depends upon it! When in doubt, use the following rule of thumb: *Underpromise and overdeliver.* Everything!

For example: If you know that your product, service, or solution takes a full two months to install and start up, then you should make a habit of quoting *ten* weeks. When it happens in eight you'll be given the key to the city . . . and if you need a few extra weeks to solve any unforeseen mishaps, you'll have them.

Now, let's look at VITO's third risk component.

Check out this breakdown . . . then consider posting it where you can see it every day.

---

ITEM THREE: OPPORTUNITY JUSTIFICATION, VITO STYLE
*Opportunity Risk versus Value*
VITOs ask themselves:
1. What do I risk losing during the conversion or ramp-up period?
2. What lag time will I have as my operation goes "live"?
3. What impacts, financial or otherwise, will I experience elsewhere in my operation?

---

### *Now Ask Yourself . . .*

How can you make a compelling case that the risks in this area are worth taking? What, specifically, are those risks? Who has to be taught what? What can be done to eliminate the risks associated with the inevitable "learning curve" associated with doing something in a new way? What have your other customers experienced . . . and what have you *and* your customers learned about managing the risks of implementation?

Let's face it. Most of the time, when you sell *your* stuff, you're replacing someone *else's* stuff. Whenever this happens there is the risk of your customer's losing some kind of opportunity. This is a fact of business life, and it is a real concern for your prospects and customers.

The best way that I know to mitigate this risk is to make it your job to understand *exactly* what's happened to your other customers. What happened as they went through the transition . . . and what lessons did you personally learn about the best way of getting people from point A to point B?

The safest way to present this subject to your soon-to-be-customers is to calm their nerves by introducing them to one or two of your existing customers who are in a similar but yet noncompetitive market. Let your new customer get it from the source!

Finally, let's look at VITO's fourth risk component . . .

---

ITEM FOUR: POLITICAL JUSTIFICATION, VITO STYLE
*Political Risk versus Value*
VITOs ask themselves:
1. Whose feathers will I ruffle by making this decision?
2. Who will I have to answer to?
3. What career or political impact will it have?
4. Who will my adversaries be?

---

### *Now Ask Yourself . . .*

Is VITO the head of a remote division? If so, what's being used at corporate headquarters, and how will that affect the political climate of VITO's decision? Political risks may be minimal, especially if your VITO is highly placed. Then again, these risks can be far reaching, and my experience has been that they have a nasty habit of hitting you on the back of the head when you least expect it.

For example, Emerson Electronics was a competitive stronghold of ours when I was selling Hewlett Packard computers. A small manufacturing division of Emerson was in my territory; Ed, the rep before me, was successful in selling into the account, in large measure because the divisional president was a bit of a nonconforming rebel.

Two years later, on my watch, he left the company and corporate put one of "their people" in charge of the division. The result: My system was yanked out. That meant no add-on business, and under-quota performance for yours truly for the first six months of the year!

The problem wasn't entirely attributable to my inability to navigate the political waters. But the fact of the matter was, my chief ally left without my having built up a new one anywhere in the organization—a problem that I could have avoided. I lost a lot of business, which was just what I *didn't* need to have happen. Neither do you.

## VITO'S VALUES

From VITO's perspective it makes little to no sense to create a business relationship with just any individual or organization . . . even if the payoff on paper is high.

For example, why would VITO want a supplier or business partner who is unethical or who shares different core business values? They wouldn't.

This brings up the question: What are the basic core values that VITOs look for? There are, in my experience, two ways to find out:

1. Ask VITO.
2. Take a very close look at who VITO has current business relationships with.

Here, for whatever it's worth, is my own short list of likely VITO values that I have personally obtained from the VITOs I have sold to:

- Unflappable trust          _____
- Unshakable loyalty         _____
- Congruency/honesty         _____
- Vigilant accountability     _____
- Due diligence              _____
- _____
- _____

The blank lines that you see are not typographical errors. They are places to write down what you'll be finding out by taking the following step:

Take a moment right now and walk down the hall, or pick up your telephone and call your own CEO, president, or owner, and ask him or her the following simple but profound question:

> *"What values do* you *look for in the individuals and/or organizations* you *decide to do business with?"*

Compare and/or add their answers to what is listed above.

Later on in this book, you'll learn how to present your organization's key values to your prospects and customers.

Before you continue with the book, take the time to visit www.gettingtovito.com and click on this chapter's online assets to get your for-free and for-fee additional information.

# 5

## WILL THE REAL VITO PLEASE STAND UP?

> **VITO Principle #5: VITOs, like eagles, are always at the top.**

In just about every seminar I teach, someone will ask: "What's the typical title of a VITO?"

That's an important question. If you're going to take the time and effort to make contact—by creating some sort of correspondence "wave," or by picking up the telephone to make a call, or by navigating through the various gatekeepers—you'll want to make sure you're focusing all your efforts on the right VITO person!

In the past I have suggested such titles as

CEO

President

Owner

Executive vice presidents (it's plural because they come in many, many different titles)

Vice presidents (ditto)

CIO

CTO

COO

CFO

(and any other C title you care to add)

Eventually, I boiled all that down to a shorter list:

CEO

President

Owner

And then I boiled it down even more:

CEO

You can choose whichever list you like. Whenever I reviewed one of these lists with my students, bless their hearts, they would say: "Tony, the CEO isn't going to get involved in the decision to buy _____."

And you know what? They were right! A CEO isn't going to get involved in the decision to buy _____ (fill in the blank with whatever you sell).

However, VITO (and, yes, that means a CEO) *will* get involved with what your product, service, and/or solution has the possibility and capability of *doing*.

*VITOs buy results—not products!*

But back to the topic at hand—how to effectively pinpoint who the real VITO is.

## SEEING IS BELIEVING

During my seminars, my answer to the inevitable, and all-important, question "Who is VITO?" involves using what I call a word picture. It sounds like this. "Picture, if you will," I tell my audience, "a telephone pole. Got it?"

Everybody nods Yes. They are now looking at a telephone pole in their mind's eye.

Then I ask, "Okay—how many tops does it have?"

Answer: one!

Picture the person sitting at the top of that telephone pole . . . and you've got VITO.

If a prospect organization has a president and a CEO, target your first approach on the CEO. Why? Because, generally speaking, the higher up you go in any organization, the less busy people become! To prove the point, all you have to do is take a look at your own organization.

Furthermore, the higher up in any organization you go, the more informed people become. And you know what else? The higher up in any organization you go, the more powerful people become.

So here's my question to you: Why on earth wouldn't you want to start by contacting the most informed, powerful, and available individual? Besides, everything picks up speed when it goes downhill. Consider this true story.

I sent my VITO letter to the CEO of the largest telecommunications company in the world. When it came time to follow up on my letter by making a phone call, as I had promised in the text of the letter, I picked up the phone and dialed the company's number, and then navigated my way through the voice mail system to the CEO's extension. To my utter amazement, the CEO answered his own phone! He was completely unprotected by his gatekeeper!

I took a quick, deep breath and started talking. The CEO's interruption came early and fast. His voice was firm and friendly:

"I saw your letter. You've got the wrong guy. I've got three different divisions, and maybe one of my three leaders might have an interest in what you've got to offer."

I said, "Great idea! Mr. VITO, would you please do me a personal favor?"

Sounding a bit guarded, he said, "What's on your mind?"

With purpose and conviction, I said, "Would you please have someone on your staff send a copy of my letter to each of the three divisional leaders you just mentioned?"

"I'll make sure it gets done," he said. VITO actually sounded relieved! He also sounded like he was quickly losing interest and patience, which was par for the course.

"Thank you for your time and interest," I said. "I'll follow up directly with your divisions. Have a great rest of the day."

I waited for the VITO to hang up the phone, and then I did three cartwheels across my office. After that, I picked up the phone and called my mother and told her she had raised the greatest salesperson in the free world!

At the end of that same business day I called again. This time I specifically asked for VITO's personal assistant.

The assistant said, "Mr. VITO's office, this is Tommie. May I help you?"

"Good afternoon," I said. "This is Tony, Tony Parinello. A few hours ago I had a brief conversation with Mr. VITO, your CEO. He said that he would do me a personal favor and have a correspondence that I sent him forwarded to your three divisional leaders. Would you like for me to fax you a fresh copy of that letter?"

"Mr. VITO already gave it to me," she said. "The letters are on their way."

"Great," I said. "Thanks for your help. I mentioned to Mr. VITO that I would be following up directly with each person. Could you please give me their contact information?"

"Give me your e-mail or fax number," said the assistant. "I'll send all of it to you."

Okay. Now it's the next business day. Imagine you're a divisional leader at that company, and you're sitting at your desk. The incoming mail is separated into two very distinct piles, regular mail and internal mail, and there sitting in the internal mail pile is an envelope from your CEO. Wouldn't you open that letter from your CEO before you paid even the slightest attention to any other piece of correspondence on your desk?

Sure you would. And so did they.

My initial calls to each divisional leader started out with me saying: "Your CEO, Mr. VITO, has referred me to you. My name is Tony, Tony Parinello. . . ." And the rest, as they say, is history.

That year I booked the largest order in the history of my company with that telecommunications company. I can guarantee you that I would not have done that if I had started my sales process with the head trainer at that organization's training center.

### *The Moral of the Story . . .*

When in doubt as to who the real VITO is . . . *aim so high you know it's too high.* The greatest power in the sales world is to be shunted to a lesser authority from a higher authority—especially when the higher authority is a CEO or some other version of Top Banana.

(P.S.: Don't worry—later on in the book, I'll walk you through how to compose the right wave of correspondence to reach VITO, and also how to conduct yourself once you reach VITO on the phone.)

Before we push on to the next chapter, if you're feeling a bit overwhelmed and are in need of some coaching, take a moment to visit www.gettingtovito.com and click on VITO Coaching.

# 6

---

# VITO's VITO

> **VITO Principle #6: Every VITO has a VITO.**

VITOs really do take direction from those individuals who are higher up in the food chain.

I know what you're probably thinking: "Hold on, Tony . . . what about that telephone pole metaphor? Didn't you say that only one person can occupy the top spot?"

Well, let me introduce you to three groups of individuals who sit on top of a higher telephone pole (as it were):

1. VITO's board of directors
2. VITO's advisory board
3. VITO's current investors

## VITO'S BOARD OF DIRECTORS

Before you think to yourself, "this doesn't apply to me," think again! VITO Inc. does not necessarily have to be traded on any stock exchange to have a "board of directors" that they answer to. VITO may have a board of advisors or investors that he or she must answer to. And if none of this applies to what you're selling today or who you're selling it to, tuck this powerful tactic away in your sales toolbox for later use or offer it up at your next sales meeting for your peers to benefit from. Just one more reason you'll get the Most Valuable Player of the Year award! *This* year!

And we also know the following powerful facts about anyone who sits on a board:

1. Board members are constantly looking for new ideas to present at the next board meeting.

   *Who doesn't want to be considered forward thinking in the eyes of their contemporaries?*

2. Board members want to be a hero in the eyes of other board members.

   *Peer recognition is one of the greatest motivators in the world!*

3. Board members are always looking for ideas to benefit their own companies.

   *Individuals at the top are always looking for new ways to do just about everything.*

4. Board members always wait until the last minute to review any information for the upcoming board meeting.

   *These folks are comparable to the business editor of a popular business journal. They're always running at full bore to meet some sort of deadline.*

5. Board members are busy running their own organizations.

   *They are the kings and queens of activity. They live in a time-compressed world. Each and every one of their days is jam-packed with action items that demand their attention.*

6. Board members are typically "C"-level leaders themselves.

   *It's quite doubtful that you'll find a member on any board with a title like "senior buyer."*

7. Board members are sometimes paid to attend meetings, but more often than not they are given a small amount of stock for their participation.

   *These folks love building their stock portfolios. To these individuals stock is gold, especially when they can have direct influence over the goals, plans, and objectives of the company they are stockholders in.*

## VITO'S ADVISORY BOARD

An advisory board is typically less formal than a board of directors. The voices of these individuals, however, are no less powerful than the voices of the board of directors.

Keep in mind that members of any advisory board are selected for their expertise. For example, a pharmaceutical start-up may invite several scientists, several board-certified pharmacists, the VP of marketing of a public relations firm, and a COO of a well-established pharmaceutical manufacturer to sit on its advisory board. Why such a diverse group? Well, the board of advisors is selected for the purpose of servicing the organization's current and near-term future needs. The members will change as the company grows and accomplishes its operational and developmental goals. Typically, the individuals who sit on an advisory board will:

1. Be highly focused on a single clearly defined career. (In other words, they do not fall into the category of "jack of all trades.")

   *Members of an advisory board are selected for their specific talents. They are typically specialists in niche areas.*

2. Be asked to bring specific talents, ideas, and resources to each meeting.

   *Typically, they are selected with a specific set of tasks in mind.*

3. Be asked to perform certain tasks between advisory board meetings.

   *These individuals need to be available on a moment's notice to assist with the job at hand, and typically they are called in to departmental meetings or asked to review documents and projects pertaining to current operations.*

4. Be asked to consult directly with other members in the organization.

   *Unlike members of a board of directors, who typically interact only with the CEO and president, advisory board members can be found working directly within the departments of their expertise. The advisory board is akin to a mentoring program, where like-to-like best practices advice is shared and nurtured.*

## VITO'S CURRENT INVESTORS

Perhaps the most respected of these three categories is the investor.

I'm not sharing any deep, dark secrets here. In the world of business, cash is king . . . and it always will be! Investors take the risk, they show up with their checkbooks in hand, and they have top-of-mind awareness from VITO.

Smart VITOs are extremely concerned with the opinions of their investors; smart VITOs want to make sure that they can go back to the well when the time comes to do so.

Typically, investors will:

1. *Not* be involved with the day-to-day operations in the same way that the advisory board member is.

   *Certain investors are sometimes known as "silent partners"— all but invisible to anyone outside VITO's trusted circle.*

2. Be affiliated with organizations that spend their time and money doing nothing but investing in promising organizations.

   *It would be well worth your time as a salesperson to know the whereabouts of these organizations and who the players are. They are connected at extremely high places in the business community that you are selling to.*

3. Be very interested in any ideas, methods, strategies, and tactics that will benefit the top, middle, and bottom line of any organization they have invested in.

   *An investor is sincerely interested in making every effort to get the biggest return on their investment. They are always looking for new ideas that will help make that happen.*

### WHAT'S IT ALL ABOUT?

Now, then, what has all of this talk about boards and investors got to do with you and overachievement of your sales quota?

Potentially . . . EVERYTHING! But be advised that winning these constituencies over to your side is going to require a different approach to the job of selling, and a different way of looking at your territory and the organizations that are in it.

### CHANGE THE TRACK ON YOUR MP3 PLAYER

As I mentioned earlier (just in case you dropped in at this point in the book), to develop my *Wall Street Journal* best-selling book *Think and Sell Like a CEO* I interviewed over 100 VITOs to learn exactly how they think and sell! To prepare for this daunting task, and to make the editing process as manageable as possible, I created a streamlined form with 15 different questions that I would be asking each CEO, president, and owner. One of the questions was:

*Who has the power to interrupt you from your busy day and stop whatever you're doing so that you take their call?*

Here was the most popular answer:

*One of my board members.*

And here was the second most popular answer:

*My mother (please, let's keep this between you and me).*

Clearly, board members carry tremendous weight. When you're in the same league as Mom, you're in the big time.

VITOs will drop what they're doing when a board member calls. Consider that the opposite of this scenario is also true. In other words, any board member will immediately recognize the name of the CEO, president, and/or owner of any organization that they sit on the board of and will take that person's call instead. Keep this in mind . . . we'll put it to use by the end of this chapter.

## A NOT SO TYPICAL DAY

Imagine a CEO at his or her desk, holding a printout and scanning it closely. The telephone rings, interrupting the CEO's review of first-quarter sales results.

Suppose that CEO picks up the phone and hears an unfamiliar voice saying, "One of your board members, Matt Talksalot, thought you'd be interested in an idea that fifteen other CEOs here in the Ohio Valley are using to shorten their time to market while cutting nonvalue expense. What's more—"

The CEO interrupts with "How do you know Matt? And what's this idea all about?"

Whoever that unfamiliar voice was just hit getting-to-VITO pay dirt. (You can always tell when things are going well during a conversation with VITO: You get interrupted—in an engaging way.)

## THE NEW PATHWAY TO VITO'S OFFICE

If you follow my advice, you'll find yourself getting appointments with every VITO in your territory who happens to have a board of directors, board of advisors, or investors. By my count, there are two ways of pulling this off:

1. Go it alone (also known as *the hard way*)
2. Use your infrastructure (also known as *the easy way*)

I'm a big believer in making things as easy as possible. Let's take a look at number two, shall we?

### *Use Your Infrastructure*

Take this book and run (do not walk) into the office of at least one of the following people:

- Your sales manager
- Your area sales manager
- Your VP of sales
- Your CEO
- Your president
- Your company's owner
- Each of your own company's board members

Read the following three-step procedure to the occupant of this office, and then discuss it in detail.

*Step One:*
Get a list of ALL current customers.

*Hint:* I am not just talking about *your* customers. I am talking about *ALL* of your organization's customers. If that list is too large or for some lame reason isn't available, then settle for the customers in your office, area, and/or region.

*Step Two:*
Create a sublist of all current customers that have a board of directors and/or board of advisors.

*Hint:* The fastest way to find out if any of your customers has a board is to call your contact and ask them the following questions:

1. "Do you have a board of directors and/or board of advisors?" If the answer is Yes, then proceed to question two:
2. "Could you please tell me who sits on it and what companies they work for?"

*Special hint:* Most organizations are proud of who's on their board and the companies they work for. This information is widely publicized and not at all difficult to get your hands on. It may even be on the Internet or in the company's annual report.

How can you get an annual report? Buy one share of stock, call a broker, call the target organization's public relations department, visit their web site (and download it—duh!).

*Step Three:*

Take your answer to question number two above, and then separate the list of names and companies into respective sales territories for yourself and your fellow salespeople. Review your own list closely and ask yourself the following questions:

- "What would happen if I were to get the help of my sales manager/area sales manager/VP of sales/CEO/president/owner in developing and sending an interesting wave of correspondence to the people I've identified on this list?
- "What would happen if I were to get the help of my sales manager/area sales manager/VP of sales/CEO/president/owner in picking up the telephone to reach out to and/or initiate an in-person meeting with the individuals on this list?"

(Is your conversational companion still listening? Great! Don't stop here—share the next chapter, too!)

# 7

## WHAT YOU AND VITO ALREADY HAVE IN COMMON

> **VITO Principle #7: The older you get, the younger VITOs get.**

When I started selling to VITO, the CEOs, presidents, and owners I met were all quite a bit older than me. At first, it was quite a job to take a seat across from these folks and pretend that I, a mere mortal, could, you know, actually engage them in conversation!

I remember being more than a little intimidated by their age, knowledge, wisdom, and business savvy. I'll admit it: There were times when I was downright paralyzed with fear at the prospect of meeting them! And I think any salesperson who's honest about what it takes to become comfortable with the process of contacting high-level people would say the same thing. The first few meetings can be tricky!

I'll never forget the time I booked an in-person meeting with the dean of schools at Palomar College. My company had just introduced a new piece of software for the educational market, and I was sure that the college could benefit from the value it could deliver. What better way to tell my story than to meet with the dean?

One week prior to my scheduled meeting, fear began to well up inside me. The little voice inside my head started saying: *"Tony, are you nuts? You don't even have a college degree . . . what are you going to tell this dean of schools that he doesn't already know? If you had half a brain you'd cancel that meeting and call on the IT dweeb instead!"* (By the way, *dweeb* is an acronym for Deals With Esoteric Engineering Bulls--t.)

I was getting very, very freaked out about that meeting, and I even thought about canceling it. I didn't, though. Thank God.

No, I didn't make the sale. But I did learn the lesson of a lifetime.

### A FEW DAYS BEFORE THE MEETING . . .

I had stomach cramps. I kept thinking to myself, what the heck am I going to say to this highly educated, intellectually astute guy? What if I make a total fool of myself? What if he asks me about my formal education? How can someone who barely made it out of high school offer anything to someone who has several degrees on the wall and a bunch of letters behind his name?

### THE MORNING OF THE MEETING . . .

I got out of bed. I was much too nervous to eat. I bolted out the door for my appointment with destiny. I arrived a few minutes early and was escorted into the dean's inner sanctum.

As I sat there, looking at the multitude of framed diplomas proudly displayed on the walls and at all the books and manuscripts on the shelf whose *titles* I couldn't even understand, I started focusing on the one critical question that had suddenly settled into my brain:

*"How the hell do I get out of here?"*

Then an idea hit me. Maybe I didn't *really* have to get out of here after all. There were other options, options I hadn't considered.

After I thought for a while, I came up with one.

"How about if I just faint?" I thought to myself.

But as luck would have it, it was at that very moment a tall, mature, confident-looking gentleman strode into his office and said in a soft, friendly voice: "Good morning, Tony . . . Richard Hamilton, pleased to meet you."

I stood up and extended my hand. As we shook hands, I came clean. "Mr. Hamilton, I have to admit—I am so nervous about meeting with you! I've got stomach cramps. This is the very first time I've ever been on a college campus . . . I don't know anything about your business . . . I don't have a degree . . . This whole week, I've been trying to think of ways I could get away with canceling this meeting!"

The dean suddenly raised his hand as if to say "enough."

It was a strange gesture—a gesture, I thought to myself, that could not bode well for me. Out of sheer, stark fear, I stopped talking.

Then Richard spoke. "That's interesting, Tony . . . I was so nervous about meeting *you* that *I* almost canceled this meeting. You see, I am embarrassed to say I don't know a thing about computers!"

We both laughed. He motioned for me to have a seat. We spent the next two hours talking about his needs and my computers. I never sold him a damned thing . . . but as a result of that meeting I learned an important fact about getting to VITO:

*No matter how big, smart, wise, popular, established, successful, wealthy, or intimidating someone may appear to be, I can still share something with that person that he or she will find valuable.*

And you can, too!

## VITO: THE NEXT GENERATION

As my sales career progressed, I noticed something interesting. VITOs started getting younger. After a while VITO and I were the same age, and now, after a quarter century of selling, I find that a fair number of VITOs are younger than I am!

I wonder if that's all demographics or if there's some other factor at work.

As I've recalled all the different business relationships I've had with top executives over the years, I've picked up on something else that's interesting about VITOs. Regardless of my age, and no matter how old or how young any given VITO happened to be, VITO and I always—repeat, *always*—shared two important traits. These two traits were inevitably common denominators that helped make the first meeting (and all subsequent meetings) move along fairly smoothly, because they allowed VITO and I to identify and discuss at least two things we had in common.

That made bonding with VITO a lot easier.

The two traits were (and are):

1. VITO and I are both deadly serious about our careers.
2. VITO and I both have a deep appreciation for the art of selling.

If you stop and think about it, I think you'll see that *you* and VITO have exactly the same two characteristics in common!

Regardless of any external differences in age or experience or education, you really do have significant shared interests and outlooks with the VITOs you'll be reaching out to and meeting with. And as my experience with the dean suggests, odds are good that you also have value to add to their day, value that they're going to be eager to hear about!

So that's the good news. Walking in the door, you've already got a lot in common with VITO without even trying.

Now, the bad news.

Hold on . . . wait a minute. Let me double-click on this. Okay, never mind. Actually, there *isn't* any bad news.

Really. There isn't. In this chapter, you saw that you can have areas of expertise that VITOs want to take advantage of. And you also saw that you have two huge advantages when it comes to establishing rapport with VITO, namely a common interest in high achievement and an appreciation for what it takes to sell something in the real world.

In the next chapter, you'll find . . . only more good news. That's a promise. Specifically, you'll find that there are a bunch of success traits that VITOs display—success traits that are tough for most people to imitate but that turn out to be very *easy* for salespeople to incorporate in their lives. The better a job you do of learning these traits and putting them to work in your career, the more you'll have in common with VITO, and the easier your relationship with VITO will be.

Aren't you a little bit curious to learn what you *could,* with very little effort, have in common with the most important person in the organization? Sure you are.

Turn the page and find out.

# 8

---

# WHAT YOU AND VITO *COULD* HAVE IN COMMON

**VITO Principle #8: VITO is as VITO does.**

Ready for an eye-opener? Recent studies have shown that a full two-thirds of the individuals running companies today in America were once salespeople! I have a hunch the other one-third couldn't possibly have gotten to the top of their respective organizations without understanding the importance of the sales process.

In the last chapter, you found out what you and VITO already have in common, without even trying. Let's take a look at the characteristics that you and VITO *could* share, with very little effort on your part. (How do I know? You may already be making a habit of some of this stuff.)

### VITOS FOCUS ON BIG DEALS . . . SO SHOULD YOU

It's a simple fact of sales life: It frequently takes us just as long to sell a small deal to a small company as it does to sell a big deal to a big company . . . and sometimes it takes longer! The only significant difference is the size of your commission check.

### *My Advice*

Take a good look at your territory and make a conscious effort to focus on the organizations that can and do buy big. That means approaching *mostly or exclusively* larger companies and contacting the top dog—you guessed it, VITO.

Any other choice will yield smaller-than-desired commission checks and longer-than-necessary time frames for you to go from your current level of income to something that will put into the early retirement category.

### *Your Action*

Ask yourself: Who do you know who is selling similar products, services, and solutions in your own organization . . . and is consistently in the quota club? Find that person, call that person, and ask him or her *who* they chase down in their territories. Don't ask them *how* they chase down the opportunities. (You'll learn plenty of ways to do that in this book. Then you can call them and return the favor by sharing some tactics of your own.)

When you're done reading the last chapter in this book, dive head-first into the Appendix that details the template of ideal prospects (TIP).

Tie your THINK BIG attitude into your daily sales routine by posing the following BIG questions.

Before each sales call, ask:

- *Would my own CEO call on this person?* Be honest! Keep your target suspect/prospect's title in mind!
- *Would my own CEO consider this company a key account?* Don't kid yourself. Your own CEO knows that bigger really is always better.

After each sales call, ask:

- *Did I ask the types of questions that my CEO would ask?* If not, what should you have asked?
- *How would my CEO forecast this opportunity?* Tell the truth, now. Is it real? Or is it wishful thinking?
- *How would my CEO follow up on this opportunity?*

## VITOS KICK THE COMPETITION'S ASSETS . . .
## SO SHOULD YOU

VITOs live their lives by the following mantra:

*Second place is the first loser . . . Second place is the first loser . . .*

VITOs live by the rules. (They also *make* the rules, but that's a different story.) The point is, they play the game fairly. Real, live VITOS will outwork, outsmart, outthink, outperform, and out-maneuver their competition, time after time.

So: How close do you come to hitting that standard?

### *My Advice*

Your competition is the enemy. Keep that in mind.

Learn as much as you possibly can about your competition. No, I'm not talking about the obvious stuff. You know that already: their products, their pricing, their marketing, blah, blah, blah. *Everyone* knows that stuff. What's really important for you is *how* they sell. What does their sales process look like? What sales training have they been using? Who are they calling on (as in, what titles)? What companies are they calling on? Who is your competition's VP of sales? Where did he or she come from? Who is their VITO? What's *that* person's background?

### *Your Action*

1. Identify your biggest competitors.
2. Send an e-mail to every salesperson in your organization and every salesperson you personally know. Find out how many of these folks have worked for your competition. Chances are, someone in your own ranks came from their ranks. Pick that person's brains.
3. Get in touch with as many VPs in your own company as you can. Ask them if they know anyone who works for your major competition and/or whether they themselves have worked there. Pick that person's brains, too.
4. The next time you're standing in the lobby of a prospect's or-

ganization (or one of your best customer accounts) look through the sign-in book. Do you see your competition's name? Makes you think, doesn't it? Maybe the next time *you* sign in, you'll tactfully omit writing your company name and just write "self" under the category of company. If you really want to throw a curveball, put your competition's name as your company (you didn't read that here).

## VITOS ACT FROM CHOICE, NOT NECESSITY . . . SO SHOULD YOU

If you wait long enough to make a decision, you won't have to make it at all.

That's not the how VITO thinks—and it shouldn't be how you think, either. VITOs don't shy away from making hard choices, and they're willing to come to final conclusions. That's not always going to win them the Most Popular Person of the Year award. But it does give them the privilege of calling the shots in their own lives.

### *My Advice*

As a salesperson you have the right and the power to identify your own approach and, believe it or not, even say No to your prospects. Not every opportunity in your sales funnel is a good opportunity, and no one, not your CEO or anyone else, is going to fault you for dumping a prospect if pursuing that prospect means that you'll be selling an unprofitable deal.

### *Your Action*

Take the time over the next 30 days to:

1. Understand *all* of the elements of your cost of sales. The fastest way to do this is to sit down with your line of business executive who has the responsibility for that component of your company's middle line. Learn what parts of the cost of sales your actions affect. I'm betting you'll find out that most of what you do on a day-to-day basis has a direct impact not only on the company's cost of sales but also on your organization's overall profitability and shareholder value. Once you know the scoop,

take actions to help lower the cost of sales. Part of that effort will involve making sure that you approach the right (read: the most profitable) prospects at the right (read: a high) level.

2. Practice saying "no thanks"—politely but firmly—to call-ins that are *not* a good fit. Remember, activity does not always equate to results.

3. Take a critical look at your current sales pipeline and weed out any and all "opportunities" that you know in your heart will never, ever close. Get them out of your life. Stop wasting the precious pre-sales resources of your organization and your own time and energy on these totally dead-end "deals." Face it, once and for all: They're duds!

4. Collect all of the "opportunities" that you just flushed out of your sales funnel . . . and send them anonymously to the biggest competitor in your territory!

## VITOS ARE DIRECT AND TO THE POINT . . . YOU SHOULD BE TOO

VITOs live in a time-compressed world. You've got just eight seconds to capture their attention. These days, VITOs are more jealous of their time than ever . . . and they're awfully particular about who they spend that time with. How about you?

### *My Advice*

In the chapters that follow, you'll be given some new and creative ideas on how to approach each and every VITO in your sales territory who's predisposed to buy from you. As you read and learn, I invite you to think like a lazy person thinks.

If you think about it, the lazy person will always look for the shortcut. When it comes to speaking to VITO, the shorter your cut, the better!

### *Your Action*

Get a copy of today's *Wall Street Journal* and walk it (or courier it) into your own VITO's office. Ask your VITO to highlight the articles—and the individual words—of greatest interest. *These are the words that are likely to register with your target VITO. Use them!*

Now take that list and incorporate it into the correspondence you'll find in Chapter 13 of this book. Study the combined list and incorporate the words you like best into your verbal exchanges with VITO that you see in Chapters 16, 17, and 18.

Keep it short. Keep it sweet. Keep it direct. (More on this later.)

## VITOS THRIVE WHILE OTHERS JUST SURVIVE . . . SO SHOULD YOU

VITOs tend to look at what everyone else looks at and see what no one else sees.

That trait is the cornerstone of the entrepreneurial spirit so critical to thriving in today's economy (and tomorrow's, for that matter). VITOS have a cool way of sizing up any opportunity and acting on it. You should identify opportunities and be able to turn on a dime to exploit them, too.

### *My Advice*

Learning how to accurately and quickly put your *entire* value proposition in front of VITO is critical to your success. Don't let anyone kid you: Conveying your value takes practice. Here are some ideas on how to get that practice.

### *Your Action*

Do a test. Find five prospects that fit your TIP (see Appendix A) but that are much, much smaller than the normal-sized account that is predisposed to buy from you. No, you're not trying to sell to these people; you're trying to learn from them. Launch your VITO campaign exactly the way you'll be learning to do later on in this book— but knowing that the prospects that you're approaching couldn't really afford your products, services, and solutions. Ask each of the five target VITOs what they thought of the tactics and value proposition that you used. After you take their advice, refine your process and approach your own CEO with what you learn in this book.

After you've done all that, you'll be ready to approach a real VITO prospect. Don't forget to ask your test VITOs for a referral . . . more on this in Chapter 12.

### True Story: Practice Getting to the Point!

A sales trainer purchased the second edition of my *Selling to VITO* book. He read it and decided to give my ideas a try on the CEO of his own company! The sales trainer created a fictitious name and company, wrote and sent a VITO letter just the way my book suggests, and at the prescribed time made the follow-up call. He navigated through the receptionist gatekeeper and the personal assistant and got to VITO—his own CEO—and booked an in-person appointment. When he showed up for the appointment, both VITO's personal assistant and VITO were amazed! VITO immediately gave the approval for a $125,000 training order to roll out my program to the company's entire sales force.

*Get to the point! Give VITO an opportunity to take advantage of!*

## VITOS KNOW HOW TO CUT THEIR LOSSES . . . SO SHOULD YOU

When VITO has to fire someone, the deed gets done.

When VITO must redirect the company's efforts into a different marketplace or repurpose or rebrand their offering to their marketplace, VITO takes action.

VITOs know the difference between knowing what needs to be done and *doing* what needs to be done.

### My Advice

As a salesperson, you're getting paid to make decisions. Those decisions directly impact revenues and expenses. By the time you finish this book you'll have been exposed to the "knowing" part of the equation. The larger question is . . . what will you do about it?

Return to this book at least once a month. Review the system. Make sure you're putting it into action.

### Your Action

What I am about to share with you will change the way you think and sell. It's an easy six-step process that, when followed, will catapult you and your career from the knowing mode to the doing mode forevermore! Ready?

Step #1. Ask: "*What is happening right now in my sales career that is limiting my performance or causing a career-limiting situation?*" (Examples: Not getting that promotion, not staying on quota.)
*Write your answer here:*

_____

_____

_____

Step #2. Ask: "*How is this situation making me feel?*"
NOTE: Basically, there are only four feelings: happy, sad, angry, scared. For example, possible responses might be:

Angry! It's costing me customers and market share.

Sad. I am below quota again this month.

Scared. If it continues I'll be on probation! Yikes!

*Write your answer here:*

_____

_____

_____

Step #3. Ask yourself: "What is this costing me?" Be brutally honest. Identify a dollar figure.
*Write your answer here:* $ _____
Step #4. Now, identify *what is available now that you can use* to resolve this situation. Is there another salesperson in your organization who is an expert when it comes to trying new ideas and concepts? If there's a sale that you just lost, can you call the prospect and ask some pointed questions as to why they selected the competition and not you? Does your marketing department have any information that you could use to better prepare yourself for the next attack from your competition? The list is endless.

Take a moment now and write down just *ten ideas* for possible solutions to the problem you identified in step 1. Don't stop until you've got all ten.

1. _____
2. _____
3. _____
4. _____
5. _____
6. _____
7. _____
8. _____
9. _____
10. _____

Step #5. look at this list and identify the single most *difficult* item to accomplish. Next, select the three actions that would be the *easiest* for you to accomplish. Finally, arrange the remaining six in order of difficulty, with the least difficult first.

Step #6. Make a personal commitment to tackle the easiest three action items within the next *five* business days.

Make a personal commitment to tackle the six action items you prioritized at some point in the next *fifteen* business days.

Finally, make a personal commitment to tackle the most difficult item on the *twenty-first business day after you complete the list, no matter what.*

If you're eager to walk VITO's walk . . . and not just talk VITO's talk . . . you will complete this exercise before moving forward in this book.

## KEEP YOUR COMMITMENTS!

The process that you just completed has been used by the most accomplished professional business coaches in America; it has been refined, tested, and proven over the years with many a top sales performer.

This process will help you build your ability to move from knowing to doing. It will help you send accurate confidence signals to your brain. It will move you from the realm of the average salesperson to the realm of VITO.

If you would like the help of a real, live professional coach in any aspect of *Getting to VITO,* visit www.gettingtovito.com and click on VITO Coaching.

Enjoy your journey to the top!

# 9

---

# What's on VITO's Mind?

There are five specific results that all VITOs look for and try to measure. Right now, I want to share that list of five results with you and give you the opportunity to calibrate it for the specific marketplace and economy you're selling your products, services, and solutions into. Why bother taking the time to learn about the outcomes VITO demands, and (just as important) how you can identify exactly what those outcomes would look like in your territory? Because if you can't identify the specific areas where these opportunities exist, my experience is that you won't stand a snowball's chance in Bali of getting to VITO.

Here are the five results that are likely to be on VITO's mind as he or she considers the possibility of working with you.

### RESULT #1: REVENUE

Let's begin at the beginning. VITO, Inc. generates revenue, and VITO, the person, is always interested in this subject. By the way, *whatever* you do during your conversations with VITO, don't confuse revenue with profit. They're two different animals!

Revenues can come from several different sources: product, service, and solution sales arising from meetings with new and existing customers; Internet sales; recurring service contracts; consulting projects; outsourcing work for other companies; and so on.

### *Your Homework*

Answer this question: Does what you sell help VITO, Inc. generate revenue? Think of a particular industry that your company targets. Now think of a particular prospect(s) or customer(s) in that niche and put an "X" next to the ways that the VITO in that industry generates revenue.

Product sales to new customers       _____
Services sales to new customers      _____
Product sales to existing customers   _____
Services sales to existing customers  _____
Internet sales                    _____
Recurring service contracts       _____
Consulting                     _____
Outsourcing                  _____
Other (_____):   _____
Other (_____):   _____
Other (_____):   _____
Other (_____):   _____
Other (_____):   _____

### RESULT #2: IMPROVED EFFICIENCIES AND EFFECTIVENESS

There are many, many areas of "unintentional" inefficiencies and in-effectiveness in the workplace today. There are so many, in fact, that if you can't find an area to help VITO, Inc. in delivering on Result #2, you're probably asleep at the switch, or perhaps your organization is getting ready to post a "going out of business" sign in the front window.

No kidding: You're not going to have to work too hard to find areas where VITO, Inc. can use your help in this all-important performance arena. Notice that I am focusing on *unintentional* inefficiencies here. When you get right down to it, no one at VITO, Inc. really wants to waste anything, least of all VITO.

### *Your Homework*

If what you sell can help VITO, Inc. create greater efficiencies and effectiveness, these are the kinds of questions you need to be ready to ask VITO:

"What processes do you feel can be improved upon?"

"What processes are not currently supporting your strategic initiatives in the area of _____?"

"What knowledge is available but not being shared effectively across your enterprise?"

### RESULT #3: EXISTING CUSTOMER RETENTION

Existing customers are usually worth quite a bit more than their weight in gold.

Is VITO, Inc. losing any current customers to the competition? How many? Which ones?

Are service contract renewals falling off? Are customers voting with their feet by walking out the door and not coming back? Are previously loyal customers "disconnecting"? Why? Has VITO, Inc.— or VITO the person—made a commitment to win back any particular customers, or any segment of the market? How high a priority to VITO is this commitment?

### *Your Homework*

If what you sell can help VITO, Inc. hold on to existing customers, you have three options. Fortunately, all three are easy.

Easy option #1:     Pick up the telephone and call [the VP of sales] in any one of your target organizations and say: *"My name is _____, and we specialize in creating effective customer touch points that create greater retention and loyalty. Is this something that would help you meet and exceed your quota?*

Easy option #2:     Pick up the telephone and call [the COO] in any one of your target organizations and

say: *"My name is _____,
and we've created a unique way for organizations in the yaddayadda industry to keep
more of their hard-earned market share.
What's the best way for me to share this idea
with you and your CEO?"*

Easy option #3:   Pick up the telephone and call the VITO in
any one of your target organizations and
say: *"It's an honor to be sharing this idea with
you this morning. We've perfected a simple
yet powerful way to keep your existing customers from ever looking at another provider
of yaddayadda. What's the best way for me to
share our results with you and [your COO]
between now and the end of this business
day?"*

## RESULT #4: GREATER ADD-ON BUSINESS FROM
## EXISTING CUSTOMERS

Add-on business from existing customers offers VITO the highest-
margin business in the world. Therefore, VITO and VITO, Inc. want
all that they can get!

A hidden benefit of acquiring add-on business is the waterfall of
golden referrals and customer testimonials that have a tendency to
come your way when you do what it takes to keep customers happy
enough for them to stay customers. Then there are the increased customer satisfaction ratings, which are particularly critical in certain
industries (such as the commercial airline industry).

### *Your Homework*

If what you sell can help VITO, Inc. get all of the add-on business it
deserves, go back to any or all of the easy options shown in option 3
above, change the question as shown in the following example, pick
up the telephone, and make a call along the following lines. Assuming you're talking to VITO:

*"It's an honor to be sharing this idea with you this morning. We've*

*perfected a simple yet powerful way to get all of the high-margin, add-on business you've worked hard for and deserve from your existing customers. What's the best way for me to share our results with you between now and the end of this business day?"*

### RESULT #5: CUTTING NONVALUE EXPENSE

It's a business truism: It's not healthy to solely derive profits by cutting expenses. However, I've yet to meet a VITO who wanted to spend more money than was absolutely necessary to attain a goal.

It certainly is a priority for VITO, Inc. to cut any and all nonvalue expenses. What's a nonvalue expense? It's any expense that can be reduced or eliminated without compromising the overachievement of VITO's strategic initiatives. Furthermore, if you have an idea on how to redirect the "saved" monies to fund new ideas that will help accomplish VITO, Inc.'s mission, you'll win the Business Partner of the Year award.

### *Your Homework*

If what you sell can help VITO, Inc. cut nonvalue expense, survey your existing customers and establish the "how" and "how much" of what you've been able to do in this department with other customers. What's important to establish is that by cutting whatever expense you've been able to cut, there have been *zero* resulting effects in operational efficiency. In other words, you must be able to demonstrate that your cost-cutting ideas put no other parameter of VITO, Inc.'s operations at risk.

You now know what's on VITO's mind, day in and day out. You're practically a VITO mind reader. In the next chapter, you'll learn to coordinate what you offer with what VITO is eager to get done in the organization.

For important up-to-date information as to what's on VITO's mind, go to www.gettingtovito.com for critical for-free and for-fee additional information.

# 10

## PRIORITIZE, PRIORITIZE, PRIORITIZE

> **VITO Principle #10: VITO's focus must equal your focus.**

Okay, here comes the fun part. My personal experience tells me that month to month, quarter to quarter, and year to year the five results you just read about will vary in importance, depending on what's going on in VITO's world. The trick is to use the right result with the right VITO at the right time. This is more of an art than a science. To master that art, you need to master what I call the Five Cornerstones of Performance. Once you've done that, you'll be ready to create the pitch you'll be using when you reach out to VITO.

*Do not* skip the following exercises!

### LIST WORK

For each of the target prospect niches in your sales territory take the list below and rank the items in their likely order of importance to VITO. The accurate way to accomplish this task would be to poll your existing customers who happen to be in that niche. But what if you don't have any customers in a given area? You can always approach the association that services that niche and ask somebody there. No association? Give it your best guess. Not comfortable doing that? Just use the order that is shown below. (Trust me: When in doubt, use the list in the order shown, and it will work just fine.)

Complete the task for at least six different prospect niches in your sales territory.

*Remember:* A niche is another word for an industry category that you are wanting to sell to, such as manufacturing, retail, automotives, pharmaceuticals, entertainment, life sciences, and so on. Most every niche or industry has a standard industrial classification (SIC) code associated with it.

| *Result* | *Niche* | *Rank* | *Niche* | *Rank* |
|---|---|---|---|---|
| Revenues: | _____ | ____ | _____ | ____ |
| Efficiencies: | _____ | ____ | _____ | ____ |
| Customer retention: | _____ | ____ | _____ | ____ |
| Add-on business: | _____ | ____ | _____ | ____ |
| Cutting nonvalue expense: | _____ | ____ | _____ | ____ |

| *Result* | *Niche* | *Rank* | *Niche* | *Rank* |
|---|---|---|---|---|
| Revenues: | _____ | ____ | _____ | ____ |
| Efficiencies: | _____ | ____ | _____ | ____ |
| Customer retention: | _____ | ____ | _____ | ____ |
| Add-on business: | _____ | ____ | _____ | ____ |
| Cutting nonvalue expense: | _____ | ____ | _____ | ____ |

| *Result* | *Niche* | *Rank* | *Niche* | *Rank* |
|---|---|---|---|---|
| Revenues: | _____ | ____ | _____ | ____ |
| Efficiencies: | _____ | ____ | _____ | ____ |
| Customer retention: | _____ | ____ | _____ | ____ |
| Add-on business: | _____ | ____ | _____ | ____ |
| Cutting nonvalue expense: | _____ | ____ | _____ | ____ |

Dog-ear this page. You'll want to come back to it when it's time to pitch to each VITO in your sales territory. The aforementioned results are of primary importance to VITO.

## FIVE CORNERSTONES OF PERFORMANCE

In each and every *Selling to VITO* seminar I deliver I am asked by my audience this simple but far-reaching question: *"What do VITOs like to talk about?"*

The five results you just categorized are what you use to get their attention. But what the heck do you do once you've *gotten* that attention?

Review what follows closely. You'll be using it as your personal pick list for topics of conversation with VITO.

### *Preferred Topic #1: How VITO Feels about His or Her Organization's Time-to-Value/Result/Implementation*

If you really want to engage a VITO in conversation, just bring up the topic of time-to-value/result/implementation—then get ready for a torrent of opinions. There isn't a VITO in the free world who is happy with the time it takes to get anything done!

The key words to use in this discussion are *acceleration of the buying process* and *acceleration of the value/result/implementation process.* Of course, if you can speed up any of these things, you'll have a direct and positive impact on the amount of time it takes for VITO to realize tangible value on his or her investment of time, money, and attention.

As a general but very reliable rule, if you can shorten anything that impacts the time it will take for VITOs to accomplish their mission or turn their vision into reality, you'll earn a spot in their day.

*Your Homework*

Do you have the ability to consult with VITO, Inc. on ways to compress any element of the company's supply chain operation? For example, let's say that you're selling a user-friendly "report generator" that creates ad hoc reports for this VITO's accounting software. The tool puts into the hands of the person using it valuable, accurate, and timely accounting information. Simple enough. The accounting department will run more smoothly and more efficiently.

But the CFO is taking his sweet time performing the due-diligence part of the deal, looking at all the other suppliers in this dimension and probably a few from a few different dimensions. Meanwhile, Ms. VITO's ability to peer into her company's financial performance is suffering. What, specifically, can you do to help speed up the process? After all, she hates to wait.

In this situation, the salesperson who is "in waiting" for the CFO to make the selection would be better served if he reaches beyond his solution and starts asking some questions . . . first of himself and then of other "C"-level individuals in this dilatory prospective account. The questions could include:

- What is this prospect's end product?
- What negative impact does inaccessible accounting information have on the other areas of VITO, Inc.?
- What is currently being compromised by not having this information?

If you can put a dollar figure on what the CFO's leisurely approach is costing VITO, Inc. you've got the beginnings of a story to tell Ms. VITO, a story about improving time-to-value/result/implementation.

### Preferred Topic #2: How VITO Can Benefit from Better Teamwork

VITO spends a great deal of time and money recruiting a top-notch staff. Yet when it comes to getting the team to work together better and more harmoniously, VITO will almost always look to outside experts to help.

Why? VITO's personality style (typically that of a Driver, which translates as "gets things done . . . takes no prisoners") falls short of the mark in this area. What, you ask, has that got to do with you and what you sell?

Well, nothing with *what* you sell, really—unless you sell team-building services—but the subject certainly has everything to do with the *way* you sell! In your approach to VITO it's important to show that you and your organization are willing to work with the appropriate members of VITO's team and make sure everyone pulls in the same direction.

*Your Homework*
If you have a pre-sales support team, I strongly suggest that you introduce the members of your team to VITO's team early on in the

sales process (say, the second or third meeting). This will foster greater teamwork and exhibit your sincere interest in that topic.

What's the best way to do this? During your first sales call with VITO I invite you to mention that you'll be introducing your team members to VITO's members . . . for example:

*"VITO, in order for us to accurately estimate if we can help you [increase customer retention while at the same time increasing high-margin add-on business], I'll need to introduce my chief web designer to your CIO. What's that person's name, and how would you like for the introduction to be made?"*

To add even more value, you should have in your hip pocket the name(s) of organizations that your own company has used (or that you have personally researched and checked out) that have services that enhance team participation. Be ready to drop the name(s) on VITO. Now, that's added value!

### Preferred Topic #3: How VITO Can Increase the Value of Knowledge-Based Workers

This is both a popular and a painful topic of discussion with VITO. I've mentioned before that you won't have to look too hard or long to find *unintentional* inefficiencies within VITO, Inc. I will bet you a nickel that one such area is VITO's knowledge-based workers. VITOs know that their biggest cost of operations is typically the cost of labor. Yet they spend little to enhance the overall efficiency of these workers in comparison with other operational expenses. For example, the second area of major expense is capital equipment, and fixed and variable expense typically runs high in support of these assets. VITO is preconditioned to the "upgrade" philosophy and may even expect these regular expenses.

How about an upgrade that will allow VITO to get more out of the people of VITO, Inc.? If you raise this as a subject and talk about how you'll measure the results, the odds are good that VITO will listen carefully.

*Your Homework*
Ask yourself how your products, services, and solutions can increase the output and effectiveness of VITO's knowledge-based workers in a positive way.

Right about now you may be asking yourself, "Yeah, but who are these people? What are the titles of these workers?" Consider this: *Every* employee at VITO, Inc. who must touch information that affects the end product of VITO, Inc. is in some sense a knowledge-based worker. Don't get hung up on titles. Think about the job responsibilities—and how much information the person has to process.

### *Preferred Topic #4: How VITO Can Find Trusted Business Partners*

This is a biggie.

Let's be honest . . . even if it hurts.

Can VITO trust your entire organization? From manufacturing to marketing to sales to service and support? Does your organization do what it says it will do, when it says it will do it?

If not, you may make the first sale to VITO, but you won't get the add-on business and golden referrals that await those who deliver in an honest and up-front way.

Trust is actually pretty easy to earn when your entire team is credible. So the big question here is not so much whether VITO trusts you (and your team) enough to call you a partner . . . it's whether you trust *your* team enough to make promises to VITO that turn into reality.

Trust is a popular topic with VITO. Early on in your business relationship with VITO you can build this trust in amazingly easy ways—by, for instance, showing up when you say you will. If you tell a VITO you'll be calling at a certain time, make absolutely sure you do so! If for some reason you cannot make a call or an in-person appointment, make sure your manager or VP of sales does it for you. If you say you'll be sending something along, make sure you send it.

Following through on your own commitments isn't all that tough. (Right?) But motivating the *rest* of the team to follow through on the promises you make . . . that's an ongoing diplomatic effort.

Make the effort internally. And then think twice before you make a commitment—any commitment—to VITO.

Remember the rule we talked about earlier:

*"Underpromise and overdeliver . . . everything."*

*A True Story*

I recently met the VITO of the largest distributor of bicycles in all of Europe. In one meeting I promised that I would send him a copy of my most recent book, which I did promptly. He sent me a handwritten note. I'll quote him: "Less than 1% of businesspeople follow up. You have earned that place in my world."

*Your Homework*

Examine every piece of correspondence you send to your prospects: every product sheet, every note, every contract, every update. Make sure every single solitary syllable is completely honest and that every single solitary syllable accurately reflects what you can and can't do. And keep your promises. Earn your place in that 1% category!

### Preferred Topic #5: How VITO Can Give Greater Focus to Core Competencies

Whether VITO is the founder of the organization or a hired gun, you may rest assured that they are acutely aware of the power of staying focused on their core competencies. They know what their organization is good at doing, and they themselves avoid getting involved in anything that deviates from that path.

Although this mind-set is definitely prevalent among VITOs, it is *not* so prevalent at the lower levels within VITO, Inc. Typically, the further you drift downward in VITO's organization, the more likely you are to run into people who don't know how to focus on their own core competencies. You'll also find many an individual who would like to creatively copy whatever you can offer and attempt to build it themselves.

Over the past 20 years or so, outsourcing has become extremely popular, because VITOs have been beating the core-competency message into every available management skull. But the internal dynamics remain essentially the same. Lots of organizations would benefit from focusing all their efforts and resources on what they do best, but they don't manage to turn that vision into reality. If you're a salesperson who sells outsourcing services, let me caution you right now *not* to call on the department head whom your outsourcing service would render obsolete. I know that sounds rather obvious, but it never ceases to amaze me how often a salesperson selling human resources (HR) outsourcing will call upon the director of HR. Can't you just hear the internal conversation?

> PROSPECT: "OK, seems interesting, leave this information with me and I'll take a closer look at it." (As prospect thinks: "What a clown! I've spent the past 10 years building this department and hand picking each employee. No one's going to take that from me!")

And yet, having heard the magic words "seems interesting," the salesperson puts this "hot prospect" on his forecast at a 50% probability. No matter what the forecast says, this prospect has no intention of ever speaking to this salesperson ever again. Into the trash go the information and the salesperson's business card. And why couldn't we have predicted that quiet sabotage of our efforts before we walked in the door, I'd like to know?

Sometimes salespeople tell me: "OK, Tony—I agree, calling on the head of any department you want to replace is a lame idea . . . but how about calling one level higher?"

Let's play *that* internal conversation out:

> PROSPECT (one level higher than the target department head): "OK, this seems interesting, leave this information with me and I'll take a closer look at it." (As prospect thinks: "What a clown! I've known each and every one of the folks in the HR department for at least three years. My kids play on the same water polo team their kids do. I couldn't look at myself in the mirror in the morning if I replaced them.")

Yet the salesperson puts this "hot prospect" on his forecast at 75% probability. (Hey, we called on the decision maker, right?) Here, too, however, the prospect has no intention of ever speaking to the rep again. Into the trash go the information and the salesperson's business card.

Guess what? There is only one individual in every organization who will definitely understand and be interested in the merits of outsourcing—and that's VITO. Period.

*Your Homework*

Position yourself as an outsourcing operation . . . and get ready to call VITO.

Here's the beauty of this topic. No matter what you sell, you can present your products, services, and solutions to VITO as an out-sourcing specialist. From paper clips to computer chips, if you supply VITO, Inc. with it, they themselves don't have to think about it. They don't have to be distracted from their core competency, not for one second, if they buy from you and you do what you say you will. And while you're speaking with VITO, you can find out exactly what his or her expectations are from a business partner or provider whose mission in life is to help VITO, Inc. stay focused on what it does best.

*"Mr. Benefito, what are the top three expectations you personally have with regard to any business partner that help you stay focused on becoming the nation's largest builder of titanium yaddayadda components?"*

Now let's push on to part two—one of my favorite topics: making contact!

# Part Two

---

# MAKING
# CONTACT

I love *doing* . . . I hate *planning.* I love getting into the game; maybe that's why I am not much of a sports fan. Being a spectator has never thrilled me. But put me in front of a telephone to make a sales call, waltz me into the lobby to get an appointment, put me in front of a room full of prospects for a presentation, get me face to face . . . and WOW!

I'm living my dream.

And that's exactly what this part of the book is about. My dream. Specifically, you'll be learning what's worked for me and for the thousands upon thousands of alumni of my seminars. The key word here is *worked.* You won't be reading about any tactic that's failed. Oh, don't get me wrong; there have been plenty of blunders. I just don't want to waste your time with them, and I really want to put them behind me!

You're about to read some wild ideas, but rest assured that I'll never, ever suggest that you do anything in your sales process and sales career that I am not currently doing in mine. Everything that follows has already been ironed out and bulletproofed. Let's get started!

# 11

## PREVIEWS OF COMING ATTRACTIONS

> **Proven VITO Principle #11: Get to the point and stay on point.**

You'll recall that, at the end of Chapter 8, I introduced you to a process that many successful professional coaches use. You were instructed to pick the easiest step of any task and do it first. In this chapter, we're going to look at some easy stuff.

### A WORD ABOUT REFERRALS

Now, the easiest way of getting to VITO is by means of a referral. Agreed? And a referral from one VITO is more likely to give you a referral to another VITO.

In the next chapter you'll learn each and every tactic that will actually land you these exceptionally valuable referrals . . . but for right now, here's a killer referral strategy that will serve as a kind of preview of coming attractions.

## *Do This Now*

Get out your customer list (or, if you don't have any customers, get out your prospect list). Start at the top of the list, pick up the telephone, and call your current day-to-day contact. (This will typically be someone of a lower level in the organization, and that's okay.) I suggest that you initiate a conversation that goes something like this:

> YOU: "Hey, Joan, it's Will Prosper. I've got a quick question for you."
>
> JOAN: "Yeah, Will—what's on your mind?"
>
> YOU: "I need a *personal* favor. Do you know anyone in (the Association of Laboratory Scientists/your industry here in town/ the ABC or XYZ company) that I might be able to help in solving a problem or two in a similar way that I've been able to help you?" (*Note:* these are specific organizations that fit your TIP; see Appendix A.)
>
> JOAN: "Let's see . . . I know the head of experiments over at Creepy & Crawly Labs. His name is Benjamin Mee, but everyone calls him Buggs for short. Other than that I can't think of anyone else at the moment."
>
> YOU: "Great—thanks, Joan. Can you tell me a little bit about what Buggs is doing over at Creepy & Crawly?"
>
> JOAN: "Sure. Things are really hopping . . . They just got a big contract from NASA and I think they're going to expand their operations."
>
> YOU: "Thanks a million. By the way, could you give some thought to anyone else that you might know between now and our meeting next Tuesday?"
>
> JOAN: "Sure, Will . . . no problem."

IMPORTANT NOTE: *Do not* pick up the telephone and call Buggs. (I know, it takes willpower, but trust me, this will be worth it.) Here's what you should do instead.

*Tactical Step One*

Find out the VITO's name and telephone number over at Creepy & Crawly by either surfing the net, looking at the Chamber of Commerce directory, or using some other directory—maybe the one that your sales manager has purchased for your sales team that has dust all over its shrink-wrap cover because it's never been used.

*Tactical Step Two*

Pick up the telephone (preferably after hours), call VITO, and leave the following voice mail message in a confident tone of voice, speaking slowly enough so that VITO will understand what you say. (*Note:* all underlined words need to be tailored to your specific situation.)

> "Mr. Benefito, Joan Goodperson suggested that I make contact with Buggs Mee, your head scientist. We've established a proven track record in helping similar research labs reduce their time-to-revenue without sacrificing quality and safety. Before we make contact with Buggs, could you tell me if Buggs really likes what he sees and is personally convinced that we can help make your NASA project more profitable, do you know of any reason why you would not support the selection of my organization as a business partner? You can give me a call or have someone else return my call any day between the hours of 3 and 5 p.m. I'll look forward to your guidance and answer before I explore all the possibilities with Buggs. My name is Will Prosper and my number is 800-777-8486, that's 8-0-0-8-7-7-8-4-8-6. Thanks for listening!"

You just hit pay dirt in the two-for-one referral jackpot!

Trust me, this simple yet powerful process for getting a quick referral to VITO works, and it's fun! *Do it now!*

## CORRESPONDENCE WITH VITO

In a later chapter I'll be taking you through what I'll call the "mastery course" in creating correspondence that will captivate VITO. But let me give you another little preview of coming attractions right now.

Over the years, I've tested many different correspondence modalities, and now I can say that I've got the system down pat. If you're a

VITO seminar alumnus or alumna, I want to thank you for taking my correspondence process and putting it to good use. The results that you've created are nothing short of incredible—from getting appointments with new VITOs to making sales in accounts that you've been locked out of for years. Congratulations!

If you're new to the VITO process, you're in for a great ride. Imagine sending a piece of correspondence to a CEO, president, or owner of an organization in your sales territory (one that fits your TIP; see Appendix A)—and just a few days later receiving a call from that prospect's office that sounds like this:

> YOU (as you pick up the telephone): "Good morning, this is Ima Winner, how may I help you?"

> THE VOICE YOU HEAR ON THE PHONE: "This is Tommie in Ms. Importanta's office. You sent her a letter, and she would like to have a conversation with you at 2:00 p.m. today instead of the time you indicated in your correspondence. Are you available?"

> YOU: "Tommie, could you please hold on a quick minute while I end this call on my other line?"

You put Tommie on hold and quickly type into your CRM system "Ms. Importanta." There you see the letter you sent and all the particulars about VITO, Inc. and Tommie. (No, there wasn't another call to drop . . . you just needed to buy a little time!)

You punch up Tommie's line and say: "Thanks for waiting, Tommie. Without making any changes, my schedule opens up at 2:15—will that work for Ms. Importanta?"

(By the way, you will be sorely tempted to say, "Oh, you bet, Tommie, I am free as a bird that whole day, two o'clock sounds fine!" Don't do that. Part of becoming the functional equivalent of every single VITO you want to meet with—in this case, Ms. Importanta—means acknowledging that you've got lots of other stuff that pulls at you and your time. And let's face it . . . you *are* busy. If you play just a little hard to get you will set a tone of popularity, rareness, and urgency. And none of that will harm your cause.)

You continue: "Could you tell me, what exactly caught your interest in the letter?"

(Always make sure that you ask Tommie what's going on. Gather as much information as you can about VITO and VITO, Inc. before you talk to a VITO.)

The scenario that I just painted is a very typical one. You will get VITO's private assistant calling you. You will get one-on-one conversations and appointments with VITO. And you will make bigger sales in less time when you deploy the processes in this book.

Let me plant the seed in your mind right now for creating a correspondence that will change your sales results virtually overnight.

It is this: *Every correspondence you send to VITO must be a quick read.*

That doesn't necessarily mean it must be short (but shorter is always better). However, what you write must have several obvious entry points. So, no matter where VITO chooses to "opt in," he or she will read something that makes total sense and prompts him or her to quickly take one of two actions:

1. Move to another part of the correspondence and continue to read.
2. Make a hand-written note on the correspondence and redirect it to somewhere and someone else in VITO, Inc.

This is a classic win-win situation if I ever saw one!

### Do This Now

Print out the last piece of introductory correspondence you sent to a prospect. Scratch your name off and put your manager's name on it. (That last step is optional.)

Now hold it in your hands and walk over to your VP of sales's office. Show it off and ask the tough but necessary question: "If you got this letter in the mail, what would you do with it?"

After you recover from the embarrassment occasioned by the response you get, ask the VP to take the time to circle any word or phrase that caught his or her attention. Make a note of what the VP says to you and add the words he or she circled on your letter; add them to the list you started on p. 65.

Now take the letter, make a paper airplane out of it, and fly it off the roof of your office building. You won't be needing it any longer.

## ACCESS TO VITO

I love gatekeepers—do you?

Honest. I love the way they wield so much power. I love the way they control access to VITO. I love the way they help me sell.

In the early days of my sales career I hated gatekeepers. In those dark days of selling I would use every single tactic I could get my hands on in an attempt to get through, around, and over their authority.

Guess what? It didn't work then, and it definitely doesn't work today. In preparing to write this book I personally interviewed many personal assistants to VITO. Here's what I asked them:

*What is the biggest mistake salespeople make whenever they call you?*

And here's the answer I got back:

"They lie like a rug."

(Those are the unedited, actual words repeated by the majority of the assistants interviewed. I am not kidding.)

Here's my advice: If you're ever tempted to lie to a personal assistant, don't.

When you get to Chapter 19, you'll get the rest of the story from the people who really do, whether you like it or not, hold the key to VITO's office door. In the meantime, take my advice and put it into your daily sales work. Tell them the truth.

## CONVERSATIONS WITH VITO

In Chapter 18 you'll get the complete system to make telephone contact and in-person contact with every VITO in your territory. The system you'll encounter there is based on thousands of such calls that I have personally orchestrated during what my alumni and the organizations they work for affectionately call "VITO Blitz days."

To align your thinking now to what will follow in that chapter, I want to suggest that from this point on in your sales career you *stop talking*.

Mind you, speaking is fine. But talking is off limits.

In my studies of Very Important Top Officers, I've noticed one consistent communications trait that they all possess. They don't talk—they speak.

And when they speak, people listen.

If you stop to think about it, you'll realize that parrots talk. Babbling toddlers talk. Clueless salespeople talk. VITOs, on the other hand, speak.

According to Webster's dictionary, the biggest difference between talking and speaking is *purpose*. I am going to suggest that from this day forward you adopt that sense of purpose and do nothing but *speak* to the VITOs you encounter.

## PRESENTATIONS TO VITO

We're going to change the way presentations are made in Chapter 15 of this book. Oh, not the standard run-of-the-mill presentations where you show off your product's functionality in your demo room or where you take your prospects to one of your best existing customer sites or where you take your prospects on a factory tour. I am talking about text, graphic, and audio presentations that will be sent to VITO and VITO, Inc. well in advance of the place and time where you would typically make your presentation. We'll be using the Internet for this purpose. So between now and Chapter 15, if you've been avoiding using the WWW-dot world for your presentations I strongly suggest you visit www.gettingtovito.com and click on "Tony's presentation" to get your arms around some ideas that will forever change the way you sell.

## DELEGATION FROM VITO (AKA THE PREMATURE SHUNT)

A good many calls to VITO wind up being a "shunt" to someone else at VITO, Inc., and a good many salespeople see this as an undesirable outcome. As will become clear in subsequent chapters of this book, I see things a little bit differently.

VITO would not suggest that you speak to *anyone* at VITO, Inc. if

VITO didn't see some level of need for and/or interest in what you've got to offer. VITO isn't about to knowingly waste anyone's time—especially if that someone happens to be on their payroll.

Here's a little secret to tide you over until we get to Chapter 18:

*Learn to ask the million-dollar question!*

The next time VITO directs you to one or more of his or her direct reports, quickly ask this question:

*"If your vice president of finance, Ms. Ryan, is convinced that our ideas can assist you in your efforts to accomplish your vision, could you see yourself becoming a business partner of [your company's name] by the end of this month/quarter/year?"*

Look what you've just done! You've put the full-court press on VITO! And you know what? VITO loves this stuff! This is the way VITO *dreams about* being sold! This is how VITO would love for his or her salespeople to sell! I strongly suggest that you institutionalize that question as soon as you can into your sales process.

Okay—those are the previews of what's coming up. Now that you've got a sense of where we're going in the next several chapters, let's dive headfirst into each area. I assure you, you're going to love it.

# 12

## The VITO Referral

I saw some research a while back that indicated that people tend to establish and maintain friendships with individuals who are within 10% of their current financial position.

Yeah, I know, I doubted it too. But it's true. Check your Rolodex or your Blackberry or whatever, and then take a look at your checkbook and your savings total, and you'll find that it pretty much pans out.

You'll also find that most of us are most comfortable emotionally when we're operating in a social and economic structure that's similar to the environments we were brought up in. What's more, many of us are currently making two to three times as much money as our parents did.

Those are two interesting sets of facts, don't you think?

The question becomes: How do those facts make us feel? Guilty? Perhaps edging into the realm of self-sabotage of your own success?

Something to think about. My purpose here is not to dive headfirst into the whys and wherefores of the glass ceilings and selfimposed limitations that we choose to live under and within but rather to get all of us to think about the *reasons* we're so reluctant to ask for what we've worked hard for and deserve. No, I am not talking about that promotion or raise in your base salary (although you've got my permission to ask for that too!). *What I am talking about is getting referrals from VITO A to VITO B.*

## WHAT SALESPEOPLE USUALLY SAY WHEN I BRING THIS UP

*"Wait a minute, Tony . . . I don't need any help in getting referrals from VITO or anybody else. I ask for referrals all the time. That's how I sell!"*

Let's do a reality check on that. Remember, this is a book about VITO, and VITO, as we have seen, is a very different animal from the rest of the creatures in the business jungle.

Please write your answers in the space provided. Please be honest!

A) How many existing customers do you have? _____

B) How many existing prospects do you have in your pipeline?

_____

C) Write your TOTAL of items A and B here: _____

D) In the last 12 months how many referrals have you asked for *from the VITOs* in your existing customer accounts?

_____

E) In the last 12 months how many referrals have you asked for from the VITOs in your existing prospect accounts? _____

F) Write your TOTAL of items D and E here: _____

G) If the number in line C is smaller than or equal to line F you may skip the remainder of this chapter and go immediately to the next chapter.

### *Are You Still With Me?*

Okay, I didn't hear any pages flipping, so let's continue on our trek, and let's do it guilt free. Let's not try to justify or explain *why* we're not asking for, or getting, referrals from VITO—let's just move on to the land of referral amnesty, shall we?

My guarantee is that if you do the work that I suggest in this chapter, by the time you get to the last page you'll be ready to ask for (and get) referrals to other VITOs in your sales territory. A worthy outcome!

Oh, by the way: If you get referred to a VITO who happens to be outside of your own sales territory, I strongly suggest you resist the temptation to poach. Instead, be a team player and send it along willingly to the responsible salesperson. In due time the universe will send you a bluebird all your own. Rely on it!

## EARNING THE RIGHT TO ASK VITO FOR A REFERRAL

The quality of each and every referral you receive will be directly proportional to the level of trust you have with VITO, and that depends on your meeting and/or surpassing the expectations that you've set and on the investment both you and VITO have made in the business relationship thus far.

By the way, if you come across a question that doesn't fit what you sell, I'll apologize now, and you can skip that question. Fair enough?

### *VITO Must Trust You and Your Organization*

Establishing and maintaining trust in a business relationship is critical to growing the business and getting referrals. I believe it's possible to build trust quickly. I also believe it's hard to maintain trust over time. Let's face it, stuff happens!

*Consider this:*

Jan was calling on a line of business executives and progressing nicely in the sales process. Not wanting to throw a monkey wrench into the equation, Jan decided to hold off on introducing her terms and conditions until the sale was all but made.

The VP wanted the solution installed by the end of the quarter. Jan had promised that delivery and installation would make it with time to spare. The VP put his neck on the line by making several announcements to the CEO touting his confidence to get the job done.

Jan prepared her final quotation, placed it with her terms and conditions, and hand-delivered it to the VP.

"What's this?" asked the VP.

"Our standard terms and conditions," Jan replied.

The VP went into a tirade. "Why didn't you tell me that your T&Cs were twenty pages long? I'm going to have to get this past the legal department . . . and that will take weeks! This is dreadful!"

Dreadful it was. Unwilling to commit a career-limiting mistake, the VP went back to the incumbent supplier. Although their proposal was more expensive and not as complete as Jan's, the VP had no choice but to throw the business *their* way.

Jan lost the VP's trust and the deal.

Jan now follows my advice and gives her terms and conditions to her prospects on the first call. You should too.

### How to Build Trust

If you want to build trust quickly, ask this to-the-point question of VITO early on in the relationship:

> *"Mr. Benefito, what must I and my organization do to earn your trust?"*

Listen to what VITO says in response, and don't ever violate it.

I'll bet that if Jan had asked this question she would have heard that VP say: "Tell me everything up front. I don't want any surprises." I am sure Jan (or any other responsible salesperson in her shoes) would have taken the time to rethink every step in her sales process.

### My Story

Many years ago, during my first meeting with the president of a large manufacturing enterprise in my territory, he explained that his marketing strategy followed a recently published book, *The Discipline of Market Leaders.* I quickly responded that I had read the book. (Actually, I had taken a quick look at an eight-page synopsis published by Executive Book Summaries.) Surprised and pleased at our common knowledge of this important source of information, he quickly pulled the book from his personal library, opened it up to a particularly pivotal chapter he had bookmarked, and asked what my opinion of the contents was.

I froze. I choked up. Embarrassed and feeling like a child in school who didn't do his homework and just got nailed by the teacher, I sheepishly said, "Actually, I've only read an eight-page summary." The president was gracious enough to let it pass.

I never got another appointment, and I never made that sale.

And you know what? I never stretched the truth again.

*Think!*

Think before you act, speak, and write. Never give VITO any reason to doubt the authority and authenticity of your word (and your organization's). If you follow this simple rule, you'll be one giant step closer to that golden referral.

When you're asked something about which you don't yet have all the facts, say so. Keep the trust. Say something like this: "VITO, this is such an important issue that I want to [do a little research/reading/ information gathering] [talk to our team of experts] [get my CEO's opinion] [or whatever] for you and get it right. Let me get back to you by [next Thursday morning]." Then (you guessed it) keep your word, and keep it on time!

Being that up-front and that honest in each of your interactions with VITO will help you make sure that your trust starts to build from the get-go and continue to build over time. And when it comes time for you to ask for that referral, you'll get it almost without asking.

Take a moment to give an honest answer to this question: How often have you created and maintained trust in your relationship with VITO and VITO, Inc.?

Always _____ Sometimes _____ Rarely _____ Never _____

### SETTING AND EXCEEDING VITO'S EXPECTATIONS

Too many salespeople work a heck of a lot harder at setting the prospects' and customers' expectations than at *meeting* those expectations. This is a big, very big mistake in the world of getting to VITO. What's the critical rule? You remember:

*Underpromise and overdeliver . . . everything!*

If you estimate, forecast, imply, or promise a result to VITO, be conservative and be prepared to put it in writing.

Yes—you should create a document of anticipated results. This can be loaded with contingencies and conditions, and you should also make it clear, *before, during,* and *after* the sale, that you and your team must be prepared to do anything and everything necessary to turn your estimates and forecasts into reality. I strongly recommend monthly or quarterly progress reports—before, during, and after making the sale—delivered in person *and* on paper to VITO's office. Doing this will *definitely* establish you as a reliable business partner, increasing your perceived value and differentiating you dramatically from your nearest competitor.

Sometimes customers develop unrealistic expectations because salespeople make completely unintentional—and usually pretty vague—statements that customers choose to interpret in ways that are convenient to them. Although this type of miscommunication isn't exactly dishonest, it can result in outcomes that are just as catastrophic as situations where salespeople lie through their teeth.

Set realistic expectations. Make sure they're crystal clear. Put them in writing. Go over them in a face-to-face meeting with VITO on a regular basis. That's my advice.

### Another True Story

"We can get your entire team trained as soon as you're ready."

A simple enough statement. At least, that's what I thought it was when I said it. Looking back, though, I realize it would have been a lot more prudent for me to ask, "When would you like to have your entire team trained?"

Before opening my mouth, I should have made a call to the training center and checked availability and put a hold on the "seats" that I would need for this new customer. But, hey, who had time for that?

I was on a roll. And as a result I made a broad statement that, although not dishonest in any way, came back and bit me right in the assets.

Unbeknownst to me, VITO made a strong stand later that very day with his VP of Operations, laying down the law that all training would be accomplished by month's end and that any and all vacations of the members of the team would be suspended until further notice. The VP's push back didn't hold any water with VITO—once a VITO makes a grand statement like that, they really don't like for it to be challenged or (worse still) incorrect.

Well, guess what? Had I read my company's own interoffice memo I would have known that our customer training center was being relocated and that all classes were being scaled back for the next 45 days. But I *didn't* read the memo . . . and how important could a word or two from our training center be, anyway?

The truth was, the classes being held during that time period were already beyond capacity. Oops.

Now, here's the point. I didn't lose the sale, but I did lose the possibility of this VITO's giving me a golden referral. That possibility went right down the porcelain fixture . . . along with my credibility. From that point on this VITO firmly requested that all statements of performance and delivery of *anything* from me and my organization be put in writing. That was over twenty years ago. VITO is still the president, his company is still a customer of the company I was selling for, and I understand they still require everything in writing.

That's my legacy at that account.

Here's a question for you: How often have you achieved *all* the expectations that you set with VITO and VITO, Inc.?

Always _____ Sometimes _____ Rarely _____ Never _____

## VITO'S INVESTMENTS AND THE RETURN THEREON

VITO will expect a return on investment (ROI) for every investment of time, resources, and money with you. If VITO doesn't *get* a return, guess what? VITO *won't* return!

Any business relationship that VITO associates with financial losses (or any other kind of loss) won't typically fall into the "mutually beneficial business relationship" category . . . and that's not going to win you referrals.

VITO has to be able to witness *and measure*—not just once, not just twice, not just this quarter, but continually quarter after quarter, year after year—that an ROI is taking place. In its most powerful form, that ROI must result in an ethical and responsible increase in shareholder value. That's what every VITO I've ever run into lives for.

If an ROI *isn't* taking place, then you have to take personal responsibility for changing what needs to be changed until one *does* take place, or you'll lose the account forever to your competition— and along with the account will go, yep, you guessed it, the source of your golden referrals.

Take a moment and give yet another honest answer: How often have you delivered measurable ROI in your relationship with VITO in such a way that VITO knows it?

Always _____ Sometimes _____ Rarely _____ Never _____

## ADDITIONAL INDISPUTABLE LAWS OF
## VITO-TO-VITO REFERRALS

Now that we understand the importance of creating and maintaining trust, setting and meeting expectations, and delivering a return on VITO's investment, let's take a close look at the two indisputable laws of getting a VITO referral.

### *Law #1: Understand VITO on a Business Level*

If you neglect to do this, you'll never get a VITO-to-VITO referral. Here are a couple of "to-do list" questionnaires that will help you get this done relatively quickly and painlessly.

Understanding what VITO's organization sells is just as important as understanding what *you* sell. How often do you . . .

- Make every possible attempt to use whatever it is that VITO, Inc. sells?

  Always _____ Sometimes _____ Rarely _____ Never _____

- Make every possible attempt to talk to a few of VITO, Inc.'s customers?

  Always _____ Sometimes _____ Rarely _____ Never _____

- Make every possible attempt to purchase at least one share of stock in VITO, Inc.?

  Always _____ Sometimes _____ Rarely _____ Never _____

- Make yourself available to attend any and all of VITO's staff meetings that involve discussions of what you've sold?

  Always _____ Sometimes _____ Rarely _____ Never _____

- Make every attempt to invite key players within your own organization to visit with VITO's key players so they, too, can get an insight into VITO, Inc.'s world?

Always _____ Sometimes _____ Rarely _____ Never _____

- Meet as many decision makers within VITO's organization as you possibly can, even if they're not directly involved with your own products, services, and solutions?

Always _____ Sometimes _____ Rarely _____ Never _____

(Remember, line of business executives and decision makers have a tendency to move around in [and outside of] VITO, Inc.)

- Read and frequently review VITO's mission statement, and then send your own company's mission statement to VITO to get his or her response to it?

Always _____ Sometimes _____ Rarely _____ Never _____

How did you do?

All of that stuff is important—I promise!

You should also ask yourself: *"What other problems does this VITO have that I may be of assistance in solving that do not involve my products, services, or solutions?"* Once you come up with an area or two, you'll have to find other salespeople and organizations that can solve that need. How often have you . . .

- Introduced your own organization's key suppliers to VITO, Inc.?

Always _____ Sometimes _____ Rarely _____ Never _____

- Introduced your sister organization's products, services, and solutions (if you've got 'em) to VITO, Inc.?

Always _____ Sometimes _____ Rarely _____ Never _____

- Introduced organizations that hold a seat on your own organization's board of directors that could be of use to VITO, Inc.?

Always _____ Sometimes _____ Rarely _____ Never _____

- Introduced suppliers of your other customers to VITO, Inc.?

Always _____ Sometimes _____ Rarely _____ Never _____

- Taken the time to join a professional networking organization?

(Typically, these organizations and the individuals they represent are reliable and creditable, and you'll feel comfortable introducing VITO to them.)

Always _____ Sometimes _____ Rarely _____ Never _____

When and if you introduce any of these outside resources, stay engaged and make sure that they deliver the goods. You may also want to work out some type of "finder's fee" or "referral fee." This can be something as simple as a lead-sharing arrangement . . . you give to them and they give to you. Ah, the law of reciprocity at its finest.

This is the best way I know of to create a referral program that you can directly control and that will generate plenty of leads without the high costs normally associated with most lead generation or marketing programs.

### Law #2: Understand VITO on a Personal Level

My experience and the statistics show that VITOs whom you're being referred to will be 2.5 times more likely than total strangers to give you a referral to another VITO. What's more, the VITOs that you'll be referred to will be 40% more likely to purchase from you!

Pretty impressive numbers, wouldn't you agree? In the 17 years that I've been teaching my VITO process I've met a good number of salespeople who have been working the referral process you're learning in this chapter and have literally never made a cold call! What's really interesting is most of these referral masters are in real estate and insurance sales. Salespeople who sell "personal" products (like real estate and insurance) tend to become more connected with their customers from the get-go. That means they generate more referrals. They have personal insights into their customers' families, personal tastes, and interests. By contrast, most salespeople selling business-to-business stuff hardly ever find out their customers' family members' names, or much else. Sure, there are some exceptions to this rule, but they're very few in number. To bridge this gap and begin to cash in on a more solid referral base I suggest you make a habit of getting the answers to the following seven questions from VITO. *Please keep in mind that I am not suggesting that you grill anyone with a series of closed-ended questions during your first interaction (or any other in-*

teraction, for that matter). Rather, your goal is to accumulate this information over time.*

1. What are this VITO's hobbies outside of work?
2. What special interest groups and associations does VITO belong to?
3. Where does VITO like to go, and what does VITO like to do on
   vacation?
4. Is VITO married? If so, what's their anniversary date and
   spouse's name? If not married and living with a significant
   other, what's VITO's significant other's name?
5. Does VITO have any children? Is so, what are their names?
   What sports, if any, do they play?
6. What's the anniversary date of VITO's employment or of starting their company?
7. What college did VITO graduate from?

How often have you asked VITO about information like this?

Always _____ Sometimes _____ Rarely _____ Never _____

(By the way, make sure you capture this information in an easy-to-
retrieve way . . . you can create a place in your physical files or in your
customer relationship management (CRM) system that will accom-
modate all of this newfound data. Make sure you enter an alarm for
items 4 and 6 far enough in advance for you to send a small card or
gift to help VITO celebrate these special days.)

*A True Story for Further Edification*
Several years ago I was conducting a VITO keynote speech at the
Fairmont Hotel in San Francisco. After the event I decided to take a
trip to the lovely little city of Sausalito, which is just across the
Golden Gate Bridge. In Sausalito I happened to come across a small
men's clothing shop; I stepped in and picked out a sweater I wanted
to buy. When I gave my credit card to the salesperson he asked to see
my driver's license and asked if the address was correct. At first I was
a bit put off, but then he explained that it was company policy. I let
it go.

Several months later, on my birthday, I received a beautiful birthday card and a woolen scarf that matched the sweater I had bought from Kevin, the salesperson at that Sausalito men's store. I was totally taken aback by Kevin's attention to detail. He not only remembered what I had purchased, but he apparently got my birth date and my address from my license!

If you're wondering about the power of the personal touch in generating referrals (and anything else), wonder no more. To this very day I continue to shop at that store each and every time I go to San Francisco, and I continue to get yearly cards from Kevin. I would safely say that I've spent over $3,000 at that store.

### Create A "Fuzzy File"

A good friend of mine and an expert sales trainer, Dave Mattson of Sandler Sales Institute, taught me the importance of a Fuzzy File during his appearance on my Internet talk show "Selling Across America" (www.sellingacrossamerica.com). Basically, the Fuzzy File is a physical file that you use to accumulate any and all information you see in your day-to-day reading of magazines and newspapers that tie into your prospects' and customers' areas of interest.

Make it a point to send the contents of your Fuzzy File impromptu to your prospect and/or customer along with a small note. *Do not* include with this note any product information, hints about special sales you happen to be having, or anything else that smells like marketing and sales.

How often have you sent VITO something similar to a note from a Fuzzy File?

Always _____ Sometimes _____ Rarely _____ Never _____

### GETTING THE VITO REFERRAL

If you answered *Always* or *Sometimes* to the majority of the questions I've been asking you in this chapter, your chances of getting that referral when you ask for it are excellent. On the other hand, if your answers leaned toward *Rarely* or *Never,* you haven't yet earned the right to ask . . . but I'll still encourage you to use the following techniques anyway, while you're making a habit of the relationship skills you just read about. Why? You could get lucky. Some VITOs are master net-workers—and they love to keep their network working by match-making. When in doubt, ask. It can't hurt.

Here are some of the areas that have proven to be fruitful for me over the years for getting VITO-to-VITO referrals. Some are tradi-tional; some aren't. Put a check next to the ones you haven't tried be-fore:

*Suppliers of VITO, Inc.* _____

VITOs rely on many different organizations to provide parts, products, raw materials, and so on. If you think about it, you'll realize that many of VITO's suppliers could also be great prospects for you.

Try this:

You: "VITO, in the past [year] of working together with your [shipping and receiving] department we've been able to [in-crease customer satisfaction while lowering cost]. I've noticed that one of your key suppliers is [Finder Industrial]. Would you consider doing me a personal favor?"

VITO: "What's on your mind, Will?"

You: "Could you give the president of [Finder Industrial, Lau-ren McAllister] a call and tell them about your success with our organization—and then let [Ms. McAllister] know that I'll be calling her next Tuesday at 10:00 a.m.?"

After you say this, don't say another word. *Don't* say something stupid like "I'll understand if you can't find the time to make the call."

Just keep quiet and wait for VITO's response.

In this example the salesperson (you) makes a suggestion as to which person VITO should call. You could take a less bold route and ask who VITO knows at Finder Industrial; however, it's been my per-sonal experience that suggesting the name of the CEO, president, or owner works best.

*Outsourcing organizations to VITO, Inc.* _____

As popular as outsourcing is these days, the chances are good that VITO, Inc. relies upon some other organization for important strategic assistance in areas that are not core strengths of VITO, Inc.—such as human resources or information technology.

Try this:

You: "VITO, I've got an interesting proposition for you. I realize that you rely on [ADE] for all of your human resources departmental functions. Would you be willing to introduce me to [Jake Pearson, the vice president of new market development] over at [ADE] to see if I could be of assistance to his other HR outsource clients?"

Guess what? If VITO doesn't know Jake, I bet VITO knows someone who does . . . and who do you think that would be? I'll give you three guesses. If you didn't pick VITO as one of them, quickly turn to page 1 of this book and start reading.

Look for organizations that have multiple clients that you can serve in a special way. In the previous example the salesperson is selling a complementary product, service, and/or solution to the user of ADE's HR outsourcing services. These types of opportunities exist everywhere in your existing customer base: All you've got to do is recognize them.

*Customers of VITO, Inc.* _____

Just about every one of VITO's customers can use what you sell.

This is what I call the "happy hour" of referrals. Here's how it works:

You: "VITO, we have an idea that will make your customers more loyal to you and your [fleet rental service]."

VITO: "What's that, Will?"

You: "You can offer our service to your best accounts as an added value. We'll give them special [VIP treatment, service coverage, help desk hours, loaner equipment, complementary upgrades, or whatever] that they can only get by being one of your customers."

You may have to get some of your higher-ups to sign off on an idea like this. No problem. Just show them this chapter of the book!

*Affiliates and distribution channels for VITO, Inc.* _____

What with the rising cost of sales and the number of emerging markets that are appearing on a monthly basis, many of the VITOs you serve have elected to establish various alternate channels of sales and distribution of VITO, Inc. products. Ask yourself: "Can VITO benefit from having his or her distributors on the same product, service, or solution that I've provided for VITO, Inc.?

Try this:

You: "VITO, do you think [Mary Jackson], the [president] of your [affiliate sales channel] could benefit from using the same [CRM system] we've provided for you? They would be able to share [sales forecast and pricing information] in a more timely and accurate way than with the [system] they might be using today. Would you like to make the introduction, or shall I let [Mary] know you're sending me to her doorstep?"

(This question presumes you have taken the time to understand how VITO, Inc. is doing business! That background information will give you the edge you need when suggesting such a referral.)

*Sister organizations or divisions of VITO, Inc.* _____

Many organizations that reside in your territory have headquarters and sister companies and divisions. You know what else? The VITO at VITO, Inc. will love the publicity that comes with blowing his or her own horn and singing your praise at the same time. Giving you a referral is kind of like using you as an excuse to do so!

Here's how it could work:

You: "VITO, would you like to be the person who introduces my ideas and proven solutions for [increasing revenue while lowering the cost of manufacturing] to your headquarters, or shall I do so myself?"

If you like, you can change the words a bit and make it sound more like this:

You: "VITO, would you like to be the person who introduces my ideas and proven solutions for [increasing revenue while lowering the cost of manufacturing] to your headquarters, or shall we give that opportunity to your VP of operations?"

Chances are, VITO will say: "That's okay, Will, I'll take care of it." No doubt about it: VITOs love to be in the spotlight, and you will too!

*Board members of VITO, Inc.* _____

Take this one to the bank: many of the VITOs that you have as customers in your sales territory have boards of directors. Its stands to reason that VITO would want to introduce you to all of their board members. Why? Again, VITOs love to broadcast their successes.

Take a look:

You: "VITO, do you think that I might be able to help any of your board members accomplish anything similar to what our teams have been able to do here at VITO, Inc.?"

Take another look:

*Your own company's VITO* _____

This one's almost too obvious—but hey, sometimes you're just too close to the fire to smell the burning.

News flash: Your own VITO has connections everywhere. Have you ever picked up the telephone and called your own VITO to ask for a referral? You should! These are the easiest referrals you'll ever generate!

Try this:

You: "VITO, would you like to make a list of all the individuals you know that might be able to use our own products, services, and solutions? I'll be glad to make sure they get into the right salesperson's hands."

I'll bet that no one in your entire sales organization has ever asked that question. Why don't you be the first? While you're at it, why don't you call each of your EVPs and VPs and ask them a similar question? This is VITO referral pay dirt at its finest. And it's not going to do your sales career any harm, either.

I hope you will review the preceding ideas carefully and put them all to good use. Doing so may just be what your sales funnel needs the most: a tidal wave of VITO-to-VITO referrals that will yield larger sales in less time.

## ASK A FEW QUESTIONS

As soon as you're given the referral VITO's name in any of the preceding situations, I strongly suggest that you ask the following questions:

- Could you tell me a little about [Mr. Bigshot]? (That always comes first. Now you can pick from one or as many of the following questions as you like.)
- What is it about [Mr. Bigshot] that makes you feel that he would be interested in our ideas?
- Do you know what [product, service, or solution] he's currently using?
- Can you tell me if [Mr. Bigshot] has any of the following specific goals, plans, or objectives for the balance of [this month, quarter, half, or year]? (Now you can mention several areas that you've got a track record in accomplishing in that industry or niche.)
- What can you tell me about [Mr. Bigshot's] personality style?
- What's [Mr. Bigshot's] private assistant's name?
- Does [Mr. Bigshot] have a private line?

*And, as your final question to the VITO who gave you the referral:*

- Could you give [Mr. Bigshot] a call and let him know that I'll be calling him?

Or, even better:

- Could you give [Mr. Bigshot] a call and let him know that I'll be calling him tomorrow at 9:30? (*Important note:* Always give a specific day and time that you'll be calling, and stick to it!)

Or, if you're really willing to go for it, the best option of all:

- Could you pick up the phone while I am here and introduce me to [Mr. Bigshot]?

(Yes . . . VITO will do this for you if you ask them to. I promise. It works.)

## REFERRAL RELUCTANCE

The thought of actually asking for VITO-to-VITO referrals generates plenty of excuses from some salespeople. Here are some of the most popular ones I hear:

- It's not the right time; we're having problems with that account.
- I don't think VITO knows anyone in my territory or niche that can use what I sell.
- It's too sales-y.
- VITOs won't share that kind of information with salespeople.
- That kind of information is company confidential, and I can't ask VITO to break the rules.
- If VITO wanted to give me someone's name they'd do it without my asking.
- I've got enough prospects calling me.

With the possible exception of the first item on the list, all this chatter is a smoke screen for something much more basic: FEAR!

Some salespeople get freaked out and worry that their request will be denied and they'll get rejected. If you know of any salesperson who happens to be a bit reluctant to ask for a VITO-to-VITO referral, what follows will help them get over it.

Know that asking for a referral will:

- *Make VITO a hero in the eyes of the person you're referred to.* Many if not all VITOs love to be viewed as the ultimate networker, and they love to find ways to nurture their network. Sending you to the doorstep of another VITO is one surefire way of keeping them in the good graces of their closest network members.

- *Create a deeper business relationship between you and VITO.* VITOs love to give advice and help others. Giving you a referral is one way for VITO to feel like he or she is giving something back to you for all of the great value, results, hard work, and attention you've given VITO, Inc.
- *Create greater loyalty between you and the VITO you're asking for a referral.* It's unlikely that VITO will dump you for one of your competitors after they've introduced you to several of their VITO friends and associates.
- *Certainly, the more you ask, the more loyal VITO will become to you and your products, services, and solutions.* Whenever you're doing an account review and you present your most recent value that you've delivered, don't forget to ask VITO for yet another referral!

## THREE POTENTIAL OBSTACLES

No matter how hard you try to prove yourself and your products, services, and solutions, some VITOs may never feel comfortable with providing the names of their colleagues. Here are some of the reasons why and what you can do about it:

- *VITO may not trust you.* This is a tough one to overcome, especially if you feel that you've done your part in the "you can trust me" department. You can always try this: "VITO, is there anything that I or my organization can do to make you feel more comfortable with providing me with the names of your colleagues?"
- *VITO isn't clear about what you can offer another VITO.* This is a common problem with prospects, less of a problem with existing customers. Asking for a referral before your prospect has a clear understanding of what you can and can't do won't help your referral cause. Don't get too anxious; don't be too compulsive. In some cases asking too soon for a referral will cause greater-than-necessary delays in getting what you want. If you think you're ready to ask for a referral, you can hedge

your bets here by testing the water for obtaining your referral. Try: "VITO, let me leave you with this thought. Please don't keep me a secret! If there is someone you know that I might be able to help in a similar or even greater way, I'd love to have you introduce me to them in the very near future."

- *VITO is concerned about hearing whomever they're referring you to say something like "Why did you sic that salesperson on me?"* Try saying this: "If you like, you can call Suzanne and let her know I'll be calling. If she would feel more comfortable, perhaps we can do a three-way call or meet for coffee on Thursday or Friday morning."

Don't forget to go to www.gettingtovito.com and click on this chapter's online assets. You'll find an interesting link to a segment on one of my "Selling Across America" shows on the topic of referrals!

# 13

---

# THE NINE VITO CORRESPONDENCE ELEMENTS

> **Proven VITO Principle #13: The power of a purposeful pen overcomes all obstacles in its path.**

One of the most frequent questions I hear about written correspondence to VITO sounds like this: "Tony, considering all the salespeople you've trained over the years, don't you think that these types of letters are losing their effectiveness with the VITOs of the world?"

The answer is an emphatic "No!" And here's why . . .

VITOs read the same newspapers each and every day. They read the same magazines each and every month. They listen to the same market researchers each and every quarter. So what's going on here? Why would VITO return to the same source of information time and time again?

I'll tell you why. Because the contents of that source changes all the time, even though the format of the medium in question doesn't. The content addresses different issues relevant to VITO's world on a daily, weekly, monthly, quarterly, and yearly basis. So VITO pays attention.

VITOs are information seekers. A smart salesperson knows how to satisfy this perpetual thirst for information and knowledge.

## THE DIFFERENCE BETWEEN KNOWING AND DOING

Possessing knowledge is one thing. Taking action on that knowledge is an entirely different matter.

Here's why I mention Seemore. If I were to pick the major difference between VITO and Seemore, I would say that it all boils down to the letter *t*.

VITOs *can.*
Seemores *can't.*

Specifically, VITOs *can:*

- Make decisions
- Approve any amount of funds necessary to buy anything they need and/or want
- Empower others
- Say No and make it stick no matter what
- Hire and fire
- Promote and demote
- Take risks
- Change direction on a dime
- Get a higher-paying job if they decide it's a priority

Seemores *can't:*

- Do any of that stuff.
- (There are any number of other things Seemores can't do for you. If it makes you feel better, go ahead and write down all the "it's-not-my-job" and "I'll-have-to-review-that-with-a-microscope" shenanigans they pull to slow your sales process down. Once you get it all out of your system, come back here for the Moral of the Story, which follows.)

*The Moral of the Story:* Write correspondence for VITO, not Seemore.

### TAILORING THE LETTER TO VITO

By my count, there are more than 20 books currently in circulation that teach the reader how to write a business letter. The problem is, these letters are written for everybody . . . not for VITO. If you follow what they suggest, you'll get what everyone else is getting in terms of interest and response rates—something close to "zilch."

Actually, if your goal is to target VITO (as opposed to, say, Seemore) the situation is even more alarming. If you use the ideas these well-written books suggest with a VITO, *your letter will not even be read!* Its contents will never even be considered!

So here's my question: How does a 45% letter-to-appointment ratio sound?

How about 87%?

How about 100%?

These numbers are not just my own experience. They are the real-world results that are consistently reported by my VITO alumni. These are salespeople and other individuals who work for average-size organizations; have average products, services, and solutions; have average sales territories; and report to average sales managers.

What's *not* average is the incredible results these alumni achieved, the process they used, and the attitudes they adopted. Specifically, they knew deep within their hearts that *VITO would read what they had to say* . . . if what they had to say followed a proven pathway.

You're about to discover the nine elements of what has come to be known as a VITO Letter. Actually, you can use it in all kinds of ways, including mailing it in an envelope, but let's call it a VITO Letter for the sake of convenience.

From this point forward, you will incorporate these nine elements into every single piece of correspondence you create for VITO. Then it will be up to you to deploy what you know into the snail mail, postcard, white paper, fax message, e-mail, PowerPoint, and/or e-presentation you compose for VITO. More on all this later.

### VITO CORRESPONDENCE ELEMENT #1: ADDRESSING VITO'S NEED OF BELONGING TO SOMETHING, SOMEPLACE, OR SOMEONE

Everyone (including VITO) has the need to belong to something. That's why associations, nonprofit organizations, country clubs, and fitness clubs of all types are thriving. If you've done even the most superficial reading about human motivation and psychology, you'll recall the work of Abraham Maslow (1908–1970), who accurately defined five levels of human needs. Among these is the need to "belong and receive recognition." I invite you to embrace what I know for certain and what Abe established beyond a doubt. Whenever you create a piece of correspondence for any VITO in your territory, you *must* appeal to his or her need to belong and receive recognition.

You'll do this by:

- Always using VITO's title
- Always referring to VITO's industry
- Always referring to VITO's company
- Always referring to VITO's unique challenges

## VITO CORRESPONDENCE ELEMENT #2: ADDRESSING VITO'S NEED FOR CANDOR

Honesty is still the best policy. Be honest with VITO, even when it hurts; we've talked about this in a prior chapter too.

Never, ever lie to VITO (or anyone else in VITO, Inc.!)—in your correspondence or in any other setting. Sell from the heart, no matter what it takes. If you don't believe in what you're selling enough to tell the truth about it at all times, find something else to sell!

Selling with honesty means not having to actually say you're being honest. It must literally *go without saying* that you're leveling with the person to whom you're writing. Avoid using the following words and/or phrases and/or anything close to them:

- To be perfectly honest with you . . .
- Honestly . . .
- To tell you the truth . . .
- We shouldn't be telling you this . . .
- Our future products are top secret, but . . .
- We'll make an exception to the rule . . .
- We know this is breaking the rules but . . .

By the same token, you must be careful about generalizations. Whenever quoting numbers or percentages in any written VITO correspondence, never use phrases like:

- We have hundreds of clients in your industry (always use accurate numbers).
- Plenty of our customers tell us . . . (how many? Here again, use an accurate number).
- A lot of the times we're able to . . . (never be this vague! How many times?).

Whenever you quote a number of accomplishments, I suggest you do it in this fashion:

- By as much as X% . . .
- Up to $X . . .

When referring to VITO's competition, use relative-ranking name-drops:

- Seven of the top ten entertainment web sites . . .
- Fifty of San Francisco's largest manufacturers . . .

### VITO CORRESPONDENCE ELEMENT #3: ADDRESSING VITO'S NEED FOR INTEGRITY IN THEIR SUPPLIERS AND BUSINESS PARTNERS

If you want your correspondence to resonate with VITO and result in a sale, you've got to be ready, willing, and able to stand behind every single word that lands on the page . . . and be capable of delivering it! (This connects back to the preceding Element #2.)

If standing behind your commitments means you fall short and the competition wins, so be it. You can always come back tomorrow, next month, or next year. And when you do come back, you will be remembered as a person of integrity.

By the way, my definition of integrity is doing *what* you said you would do, *when* you said you would do it . . . and if for some reason you *can't* do it when you said you would, *speaking up* well in advance of the deadline.

Putting integrity into your correspondence is easier than you think. Avoid using phrases like this one:

- If you have any questions you can call me at . . .

That's not taking personal responsibility—and personal responsibility is a cornerstone of integrity. Remember, *you* are sending the correspondence to the recipient. It's *your* job to call and find out whether your contact has any questions!

By the way, if you follow my advice in each and every piece of correspondence that you create and send to VITO, you'll be taking the responsibility to call VITO and you'll do so using specific language, such as "I'll call your office at [8:30] on [Tuesday, May 14]." Whenever you build something like this into your correspondence, you must, repeat must, call at the prescribed time! (Actually, it's not a bad idea to call a couple of minutes early.)

You should also stay away from "Assuming that . . ." or "We might be able to . . ." or any other rendition of a wishy-washy promise or "weasel language." Individuals with integrity stand tall and stay away from conditional language.

You should also stay away from "Let me tell you . . . ."

Avoid making any recommendation or offering any opinion if you do not yet understand what VITO, Inc. wants to do. If you haven't been asked for your opinion, don't offer it. Doing so is the sales equivalent of malpractice.

## VITO CORRESPONDENCE ELEMENT #4: ADDRESSING VITO'S REQUIREMENT OF CREDIBILITY

*Cred-i-bil' i-ty: the quality of inspiring belief or confidence, a testimonial attesting to the bearer's right to be believed.*

Earning and maintaining credibility is vitally important. It starts with your correspondence and continues into the first conversation (which we'll be covering in a few short chapters). It's often said that you can't get too much of a good thing . . . and certainly that's the way it is with credibility.

There are two surefire ways of establishing credibility:

- One: Use your brand's reputation.
- Two: Use a letter of recommendation—a written testimonial about your personal performance and the performance of your products, services, and solutions.

*Important note:* Your brand's reputation is the same as saying your company's reputation.

Let's talk about your company's brand. Does it cause serious pre-judgement? In other words, when VITO (or, just as important, VITO's personal assistant) sees your company's name or trademark, is there a knee-jerk response? And is that response good or bad?

Here's my advice. If possible, use your brand *only* with current or past customers with whom you've had good results. In all other cases, avoid leading with your brand in correspondence and early conversations.

Now let's talk about letters of recommendation. When's the last time you actually asked any one of your best customers for a letter of recommendation? If it's been a while, pick up the telephone right now and call the top 10% of your current prospects (yes, prospects) as well as the top 10% of your customers and ask each of them for a letter of reference. (If you don't have any customers, go to someone in your organization who does and ask for help with this part.)

Start the process that will get you a fistful of written letters of recommendation that state just how good you really are. You'll be using these with VITO and the individuals VITO trusts most to get things done at VITO, Inc.

## VITO CORRESPONDENCE ELEMENT #5: ADDRESSING VITO'S NEED FOR RECEIVING QUANTIFIABLE VALUE

VITO demands value from all of her or his business relationships and investments. The fastest way to prove your value is not by asking your suspects and prospects to read your marketing materials but by *connecting your prospective VITO to one or more of your existing customer VITOs.*

To do this effectively, you must be able to broadcast the value you deliver to your existing customers to your prospects. Broadcasting means telling your prospect VITO's success stories. Here's what they should sound like:

- "Our widgets produced faster time to market and lower expenses for the fifth largest process manufacturing plant in New Jersey."

- "We were able to help reduce overhead costs by as much as 12% last quarter while increasing overall effectiveness for six of the top ten law firms here in San Ramon."

The implication, of course, is that if your suspect/prospect should ask to speak with someone at that joint in New Jersey, you'll be ready, willing, and able to supply all the contact information then and there.

Want to lose VITO credibility points in a hurry? When you're asked for the person's name and phone number, say something like this: "I'll have to get it for you." Or, even worse, "That's not my territory; I'll have to get the name from our marketing line of business executive."

If you're going to use any form of name dropping/referral selling/look-what-we-did-for-so-and-so to build your credibility, be willing to take the following steps:

1. Work with existing customers and find out exactly how well (or how poorly!) your product, service, or solution is actually working.
2. Once you isolate your existing customers who are thrilled with what your organization has accomplished for them, you have to quantify the level and different types of value they are actually experiencing.

That might mean someone (or a bunch of someones) has to be able to put a real, verifiable number on what your organization has done for your customer. If your customer is willing to do the number crunching for you, that's great! In many instances, though, you'll need to ask for raw data from the customer, analyze them yourself, and submit them to the line of business executive that you're delivering that value to for approval.

Yes, this will most likely take some time . . . but probably not as much time as you think. The truth is that this is work you should do for all your current customers—at least the ones you want to keep! When VITO's line of business executives start their budget-crunching exercises, don't you want to be able to demonstrate, in no uncertain terms, the value you add? Sure you do!

Why do this when you can choose not to? Because you definitely don't want to do it when you *have* to . . . namely, in an attempt to save the business from your competition.

## VITO CORRESPONDENCE ELEMENT #6: ADDRESSING VITO'S NEED FOR GREED

The power of greed is truly awesome. I have seen it, used it to my advantage, and consistently promoted it to sell to the VITOs of the world.

I did, however, at one point in my life spend a good deal of time with a small group of individuals who did not in any way shape or form exhibit a need for greed. They were Buddhist monks at the monastery in Tembochie, in the kingdom of Nepal. If I were selling to them, I wouldn't build any correspondence around this principle. But I'm not. And neither are you.

That means that incorporating greed into your correspondence is a good idea, whether or not doing so is politically correct. Here's how you can do it.

VITO will expect to get something of value for free. Count on it. By something of value I mean something that VITO and/or VITO, Inc. can actually use. Your text should cater to this expectation as directly (and ethically) as possible. Here's the fastest way to do this:

First, take two blank pieces of paper. On the first one write nonstop for a full 10 minutes a list that includes every single service, study, evaluation, brainstorming session, survey, or other service you perform for your prospects that you currently *do not* charge for. (Usually, we give such stuff away because we're trying to get people to buy our stuff.) If need be, get one of your peers or your sales manager to help out, or do this exercise at your next sales meeting.

Now, take the other piece of paper and on it write nonstop for a full 10 minutes every single service you perform for your *customers* that you don't currently charge them for. This should include: your 24-7-365 help desk, your next-day service response, your conversations with application engineers, and so on. Whatever you do, write it all down. As with the first step, get help if you need it.

Don't cheat yourself by saying "This or that isn't really important; our competition can do that too." Write it all down. Chances are your competition isn't as smart as you are in broadcasting these freebies!

Now, assign a dollar value to each and every one of the items on both of your sheets of paper. Take the grand total and hold on to it. In just a few paragraphs, you'll learn how to take that list to the "correspondence bank."

## VITO CORRESPONDENCE ELEMENT #7: ADDRESSING VITO'S NEED TO WORK WITH AN AUTHORITY IN *HIS OR HER* INDUSTRY

How important is authority to a VITO? Very important! VITO wants to know that he or she is working with an equal—someone who is an authority on the topic at hand (like VITO's industry and its woes). After all, why else would VITO bother talking to you? Nobody likes taking unnecessary risk. Nobody likes intentionally wasting time or making "unavoidable" mistakes. Nobody (and definitely no VITO) would recruit a novice as a strategic business partner!

That's why VITOs demand to work with an authority.

Here are three steps you can take to become an authority in the industries you call upon:

1. Join and participate in every single association that caters to the industry/niche or subgroups you sell to. Go to the meetings, volunteer to help, join committees, read their newsletters. Side benefit: You'll meet a few VITOs and many of their line of business executives.

2. Subscribe to the periodicals your suspects/prospects and customer VITOs subscribe to. You must read whatever you subscribe to. As you read, make sure you cut out, mark, and/or photocopy any articles your suspects, prospects, and/or customers would be interested in. (Distribute these as appropriate. Remember the fuzzy file from Chapter 12.)

3. Whenever you're around any of your factory experts or technical types, make sure to take lots of notes and ask lots of questions. As preparation for this, consider polling your prospects and customers and asking them something like this: "Could you do me a favor? I am getting ready to attend a conference call with our new product development manager, and I need a little guidance on what I should ask. If you had one question to ask

her, what would it be?" Write the question down. When you get the answer, make sure you circle back to your "donor" with what you found out.

This is a tough one, because your job is not merely to collect information but to distinguish what's meaningful to VITO from what isn't. Not every piece of knowledge is relevant to every VITO.

## VITO CORRESPONDENCE ELEMENT #8: ADDRESSING VITO'S NEED FOR CERTAINTY

Want to make a sale to VITO in record time? Establish trust and then offer satisfaction beyond a guarantee—a satisfaction conviction. Do this by reversing as much risk as you can.

We're not talking about your garden-variety guarantee here. How many times do you think VITO has heard or seen words like "free trial period" and "satisfaction guaranteed"? Hundreds of times? Thousands of times? Hundreds of thousands of times?

Now ask yourself: How many times do you think those words actually prompted VITO to take a second look at the offer in question? Hardly ever!

The key is to poll your current customers and ask them to validate what your service to them has been. What has been their level of satisfaction? What's your overall service or customer satisfaction ratings? Don't know? Find out and don't be bashful in broadcasting them to VITO.

By the way . . . when was the last time you personally *read* your product's warrantee and guarantee policy? Read this stuff and know how it relates to VITO's world!

## VITO CORRESPONDENCE ELEMENT #9: ADDRESSING VITO'S NEED FOR CHARISMA

This is all about personality—but not yours!

What's at issue is the personality of your product, service, or solution. In order to present your product in an effective way to your prospects you must be able to use the written word to explain in a compelling way the *emotional impact* of whatever it is you're selling.

You must be able to communicate your product's essence . . . its nature . . . its sizzle . . . its flash . . . in a flash! Before you move on to the next part of this chapter, do the following exercise. Remember, you're writing this for a VITO, not for anyone else at VITO, Inc. Be careful of the words and phrases you choose!

1. Put your product in front of you. (If it's, say, an antibody drug for some dreaded disease, then a picture of it will do quite nicely.)
2. Use your product. (If you don't know how to operate it, or if by operating it you would endanger your life and the lives of others—for example, if it's a portable emergency defibrillator like the ones you see at major airports—then just picture a qualified individual using your product.)
3. Now, write three simple "nature bullets" to describe the nature of your product. What is its purpose in life? What emotional impact does it convey to its users?

You're about to get a head start on your correspondence to VITO . . . by boiling the nature of your product, service, or solution down to a single sentence (or bullet). Here, by way of example, are nature bullets of *my* products, services, and solutions—written in "VITO-ese." Take a look:

- Your vice president of sales will lower the cost of sales up to 50% . . . while improving the accuracy of your sales forecast.
- Each and every initial sale will be as much as 54% larger . . . while at the same time shortening your critical time-to-revenue.
- Totally protect your existing market share and get all of the add-on business you deserve from your existing customers . . . up to 120% of your current business with them!

Now you try it.
*First bullet:*

_____

_____

_____

*Second bullet:*

_____

_____

_____

*Third bullet:*

_____

_____

_____

We're on a roll . . . let's continue to the next chapter, so you can learn more about putting together that all-important VITO correspondence!

# 14

---

# THE FAB FIVE

*Important: Do not skip the activities in this chapter.* As you make your way through the questions and exercises that appear throughout this (extremely important) chapter, I want you to avoid answering as though you were answering them for *yourself.*

Do not answer these questions and complete these exercises from your own point of view. Make your very best effort to complete the work in this chapter from the point of view of VITO using what you've learned so far in this book.

Also, if you're a *Selling to VITO* seminar alumnus or alumna, please don't skip this section thinking you already know this information. I've upgraded the course since you saw it last, and this is a completely different intellectual work! In other words . . .

*This is not a review . . . it's new!*

## GOALS OF YOUR VITO CORRESPONDENCE

The goals of your VITO correspondence are as follows:

1. Your VITO correspondence must be able to be scanned quickly *before* it's read, and it must be a quick read. So forget about long blocks of text.

2. Your VITO correspondence must be relevant to current situations and circumstances that *this* VITO is wanting some type of new idea for. So get ready to focus on *one and only one person's* problems and opportunities—that would be VITO.
3. Your VITO correspondence must be written so VITO can easily understand it and take action. No tech-talk or buzzwords.
4. Your VITO correspondence must be able to be easily forwarded to, or archived for easy retrieval at a later date and time by, *someone other than VITO.* So if the message would not be easy for VITO to highlight and forward to a line of business executive or some other "C" suite player at VITO, Inc., it flunks.

With these four goals in mind, let's dive into the deep end of pool . . . and start building the correspondence that will transform your career!

## THE FAB FIVE ELEMENTS OF A VITO LETTER

In 1995 I introduced a five-part correspondence system that forever changed the way salespeople wrote letters of introduction to people at the top. Over the years I've tweaked the model, but the letter still breaks down into five basic components.

Let's look at the elements of style for twenty-first-century VITO correspondence.

## PART ONE OF THE FAB FIVE: THE HEADLINE

Your VITO Letter's Headline sits at the top of the page, not your logo.

If your company's logo appears anywhere on the upper portion of the page, you're not writing a VITO Letter.

*Important note:* For those of you who must identify your organization by displaying its logo because of some industry or government regulations or your sales manager's rules, put it along the bottom edge of your letter to VITO.

Your logo's purpose is to tout who you are and what your company is, and at this point that's not important. In fact, in most cases your logo will run the risk of causing a prejudgment as to what your letter is all about.

Keep in mind that most VITOs have personal assistants (PAs) opening up their mail. And according to my research, if a PA sees a logo that they associate with a given product, service, or solution category that's already in place, *your letter goes in the shredder . . . no matter what it says.*

The only time you'll be using your logo is when you send a *current* customer any sort of correspondence. Otherwise, start with a blank piece of paper.

Now, back to our Headline. Its purpose is to catch the reader's attention (in this case, VITO or their PA) and to get the reader to want to read and know more . . . just like a headline in the *Wall Street Journal* or *Forbes* magazine is supposed to keep a reader hooked.

In the old days, Headlines of VITO letters could be up to 30 words. Now we're down to much less. Why? Because back in the old days of the mid-nineties, you, VITO, and I had more time on our hands. That's all changed. (Do you realize that in 1995 no one had heard of the World Wide Web yet?)

We now live in a drive-through, time-compressed, get-it-done-yesterday, have-it-my-way, click-and-point, "I am done with this" world. Therefore, VITO has even less time to read anything you send along than he or she did a decade ago.

You've got to make your Headline pose a powerful point and grab VITO's attention. Let's take a closer look at how we build the Headline of today.

This is one of those situations in our sales work where *shorter is always better*. So what I'm going to ask you to do is build a 30-word Headline and then *boil it down to a four-word "clip."* From there, you'll build a complete thought to catch VITO's attention.

Since I know me and what I sell better than I know you and what you sell, I'll take you through the following exercise using the products, services, and solutions that I sell. Then you'll have the chance to build a killer Headline about your stuff. If by the end of this chapter you feel that you would like a critique of your work to make it the best it can be, I invite you to join "Club VITO" at www.sellingtovito.com. Membership includes personal assistance on building a VITO Letter and many other mentoring and coaching services for a fee.

### Example Number One

What follows is a 30-word Headline—but notice that it was written to catch the attention of a salesperson, not a VITO. This will show you the process that I used to create a title for a book that I wrote. It's is a great illustration of how you can use this "boil-it-down" process for just about everything that needs to be short, powerful and attention getting.

30-word version:

"Increase the size of each initial sale while cutting your sales cycle time in half. Get appointments with the approver in every organization that's predisposed to buying whatever you're selling."

Cut in half—15-word version:

"Learn how to make appointments with every organization that's pre-disposed to buying whatever you're selling."

Cut in half again—seven-word version:

"Find the right place to sell quickly."

Cut in half again—four words:

"Stop Cold Calling, *Forever!*"

See how it works? Let's look at the process again.

### Example Number Two

What follows is a 30-word Headline that was written to catch the attention of a VITO for the products, services, and solutions that I sell. This Headline is *not* written for a salesperson or for Seemore!

30-word version:

"Sixty-five of the Fortune 100 increased earnings while reducing their cost of sales up to 50% in six months. Would you like to meet the team who made it possible?"

Cut in half—15-word version:

"Overachieve sales initiatives while reducing cost up to 50% with a six-month payback."

Cut in half again:

"Invest $500,000, receive 2,000% return in six months."

Cut in half again:

"Increase shareholder value."

### Now, You Try It

Take the time right now to create a Headline for your products, services, and solutions that will make sense from VITO's point of view. This is the most important single element of your VITO Letter.

If you sell more than one primary product, take the time to create more than one Headline. Bear in mind that Headlines must not only be product specific—they must also be industry specific to the VITO you are reaching out to. I know, I know, this sounds like a lot of work—but once it's done you'll be well on your way to getting to VITO. So if you sell to more than one industry, take the time and create a Headline for two or three industries.

30-word version._____

_____

_____

_____

_____

_____

Cut it in half: 15-word version. _____

_____

_____

_____

Cut it in half again: Seven-word version. _____

_____

_____

Cut it in half again: Four-word verion. _____

_____

## VITOS WANT MORE

Maybe you're thinking: "A four-word Headline isn't enough to catch VITO's interest! They'll blow off that *Increase shareholder value* Headline in a heartbeat!"

You know what? I totally agree! Truth be told, a four-word Headline just *isn't* enough for any VITO to understand the concept of what you (or I) have to offer. We must create a more complete Headline, one that tells enough of the story to grab VITO's interest without telling them too much! *But we have to use the four-word version as a starting point.*

Here's the concept. VITOs are impatient (just like you and me, only more so). You've got to give them the punchline first and then explain just a little bit (not too much) more. Take a look at this:

*Increase shareholder value, invest $500,000, and*
*receive a 2,000% return in 6 months.*

See what I did? Basically, I took my four-word "clip" and added to it my seven-word statement . . . which gave the whole Headline more oomph.

VITOs don't have the patience or interest to endure the classic, drawn-out Feature, Advantage, Benefit pitch. A Benefit/Advantage model always works with VITO. In other words, we're going to give it to them straight. *What does VITO get out of this?*

Forget the Feature(s) altogether. Follow the example I've given, and put the Advantage after your Benefit. The Benefit is for every VITO in the world the most important element of any proposition. Here's why:

*VITOs demand results from everyone and everything!*

Sound familiar?

Your Headline and everything else you show VITO must present an idea and then answer the question: *"How can they do that?"* Take a look at my sample Headline again and you'll see how it works.

*VITO reads:*
Increase shareholder value . . .

*VITO thinks:*
"How can they do that?"

*VITO reads . . .*
Invest $500,000 and receive a 2,000% return in 6 months.

*VITO thinks:*
"I better keep reading and see if there's a catch somewhere."

As a matter of fact, your entire VITO letter must take the reader, AKA VITO, though a series of presenting ideas built around answering the simple but yet so very important question: *How can they do that?*

Your writing must also prompt VITO to add a question to their own repertoire: "How can *I* do that?"

Now you try it.

Take the four-word clip that you ended your Headline exercise with and combine it with either your seven-word or 15-word statement to create a Headline that presents your idea and answers the question: "How can they do that?"

_____

_____

_____

_____

VITO lives in a time-compressed world. VITO is focused on the end of the quarter, the end of the half, the end of the year. No matter what we present, we must always include the element of time.

Understand—we're not talking about the time it will take for you to deliver, install, and implement your ideas, products, services, or solutions . . . but rather the time it's going to take VITO to realize the benefit. Take a moment and make sure that the Headline you just wrote in the space provided pays attention to this indisputable VITO law and includes the element of time.

Now do another draft:

_____

_____

_____

_____

A "buying sign" comes when VITO says (silently or out loud), "How can I do that?" Here's how we can make that buying sign much more likely—with a sub-Headline. Just add a short sentence that answers the question "How can I do that?" Put it under your Headline. Make it a quote from the VITO (CEO, president, or owner) of the organization *you* sell for.

Here's what my Headline and sub-Headline look like:

> *Increase shareholder value, invest $500,000, and*
> *receive a 2,000% return in 6 months.*
> *"Would you like to meet the team who can make it possible?"*
> —Anthony Parinello, CEO Sales Broadcasting, Inc.

Now do another draft incorporating your own sub-Headline:

_____

_____

_____

_____

_____

## PART TWO OF THE FAB FIVE: YOUR TIE-IN PARAGRAPH

The second element of your VITO correspondence is the tie-in paragraph. It has three very distinct jobs:

- It continues to pique the interest of VITO.
- It completes the thought that the Headline introduced.
- It introduces your ideas in a way that VITO can easily understand.

What you write (or don't write) in the first sentence of your tie-in paragraph will greatly impact VITO's desire to read the second sentence. Therefore the goal of the first sentence is to get VITO to read the second sentence!

There is one and only one way to do this: Keep it short!

Here again let me direct your attention to the most-read documents in VITO's world . . . articles in a newspaper or magazine. The first sentence in a paragraph in these pieces is usually the shortest one. It plants the seed and gets VITO to want to read more.

For the first sentence of your tie-in paragraph, consider using larger type size than the second sentence and/or bold typeface and/or italicized print.

Here's an example of what the tie-in paragraph might look like. Notice the short first sentence:

> Compliance will keep the feds off your back. We're working for 75 other CEOs in the finance and banking industry to ensure that the privacy and safety of their corporate records are guaranteed.

Or, even better:

> *Compliance will keep the feds off your back.* We're working for 75 other CEOs in the finance and banking industry to ensure that the privacy and safety of their corporate records are guaranteed.

Or:

> **Compliance will keep the feds off your back.** We're working for 75 other CEOs in the finance and banking industry to ensure that the privacy and safety of their corporate records are guaranteed.

Or:

> **Compliance will keep the feds off your back.** *We're working for 75 other CEOs in the finance and banking industry to ensure that the privacy and safety of their corporate records are guaranteed.*

Now let me ask you . . . What do you think the job of the second sentence is? That's exactly right! To get VITO to dive headfirst into the third sentence!

Maybe you're asking yourself: "When does this stop?" The answer is: not until we're sure we've got the VITO hooked! And how do you get VITO hooked? By continuing to pitch the Benefits and Advantages of your products, services, and solutions.

### *Now You Write It!*

In the space provided, create a first and second sentence of your tie-in paragraph. Make sure it works with the Headline you created earlier in this chapter.

_____

_____

_____

_____

_____

_____

_____

_____

_____

_____

If you need to create a second draft, use a separate sheet of paper.

Let's look at the rest of the tie-in paragraph. Be sure you use this part of the letter to make the following points:

1. Establish your credibility by posing a profound relevant question.
2. Make a relevant statement from a creditable source.
3. Segue into the next element of your correspondence.

Here are some examples that show my first and second sentences and my tie-in paragraph: Consider that these are written for VITOs, not for normal mortals. I've taken what you're about to read from a VITO correspondence that's proven to get an 85% correspondence–to-appointment ratio!

**Compliance will keep the feds off your back.** We're working for 75 other CEOs in the finance and banking industry to ensure that the privacy and safety of their corporate records are guaranteed. Collectively, we've been able to create greater confidence with shareholders, board members, and the marketplace while increasing revenues and efficiencies that provide annuities that continue to increase shareholder value every month.

### *Now, You Write Your First Paragraph*

This may seem like a lot of work. But would you rather spend your time with Seemore—down in the "bowels" of VITO, Inc., spinning your wheels and getting nowhere fast?

I thought not. Let's keep going. Take a moment and rewrite the entire first paragraph for your correspondence using your first and second sentences that you just created. No shortcuts . . . do your work!

_____

_____

_____

_____

_____

_____

_____

_____

_____

_____

_____

### PART THREE OF THE FAB FIVE: BENEFIT BULLETS

You'll find these sitting right in the center of your VITO correspondence. Benefit bullets must accomplish two tasks:

- Establish your presence as an authority figure that's equal to VITO
- Create your best selling environment

Remember: VITO loves Benefits and Advantages. Seemore, on the other hand, loves Features and Functions. Don't lose sight of the audience for your correspondence!

Make sure that you use words and/or phrases that are of interest to VITO. Doing so will ensure that you establish yourself as an authority of Equal Business Stature.

Equal Business Stature means:

- Being ready, willing, and able to play on the same level and be the functional equal of the person to whom you're sending this correspondence (this same principle applies to e-mail, e-presentations, telephone conversations, voice mail, and in-person visits . . . whatever!).
- Assuming you have the ability and the right to change VITO's pattern by initiating a new, mutually beneficial business relationship.
- Having an equal understanding of some of the problems any VITO might be facing.
- Taking the initiative to articulate your problem-solving ideas in a way that the top person can easily understand.
- Assuming the right to communicate in precisely the way VITOs do, regardless of whether CEO, president, or owner is your job title.

Here are good examples of Benefit Bullets:

- In the words of VITO Benefito, president of VITO, Inc., "an overwhelming increase in the efficiency and positive attitude of our support staff resulted in an increase of brand reputation and customer service."
- Obtain greater market share and reduce time-to-revenue by creating greater amounts of new business with prospects—in some cases up to 70% more!
- Increase customer retention and eliminate erosion of hard-earned market share while experiencing an average of 13% increased quarterly revenues.
- Reduce time-to-market expense with time savings ranging from one to six months without any compromises on quality.

### *Write Your Own Bullets*

In your bullets, make every attempt at using one or more of the following words:

Results

Value

Lasting

Goals

Plans

Objectives

Initiatives

Strategies

Enhancing

Exceeding

Achieving

Overachieving

Time

Edge

Tailor

Customize

Tactical

Solution

Increase

Decrease

Now, add the list of words you gathered in Chapter 8.

These are time-tested VITO words. Use them!

Okay, take out your pen or pencil. You knew I was going to ask you to do this. Stop whining. Create at least three Benefit Bullets for VITO right now.

_____

_____

_____

_____

_____

_____

_____

---

_____

_____

_____

It's often said that a picture is worth a thousand words. Well, guess what? So is a pie chart or bar graph!

You can use these instead of bullet points. You can also use a comparison chart. Just make sure the graphic highlights the specifics of a situation that you can solve and that VITO will understand. Your chart can depict, for instance, what was taking place before and after your products, services, and solutions were put in place for another VITO.

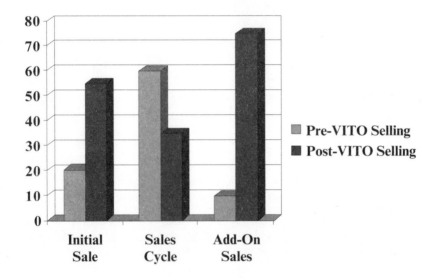

## PART FOUR OF THE FAB FIVE: YOUR ENDING PARAGRAPH

Your ending paragraph wraps up your correspondence and makes two important points:

1. It introduces an element of uncertainty.
2. It creates a Sense of urgency.

The uncertainty is very important. Basically, you're going to communicate this message: "I'm not really sure whether I could do the same thing for you, VITO."

You want readers of your letter to say or think, "Why not? Why *couldn't* we do something similar or even better?" Don't worry. This approach will not create doubt in your prospect's mind about your ability or your product, service, or solution, and it won't decrease your Equal Business Stature. It will, on the contrary, add a dose of reality to all of the prior claims in your correspondence and speed up the timelines for you.

Here are a few examples of a good ending paragraph:

- Could your company realize similar or even greater substantial benefits? Frankly, at this point it's too early to tell. But I would welcome the opportunity to learn more about your unique business needs and under your direction take the first steps to find out.

- We would value your opinion on some of our [growth management] solutions and whether they could possibly work for you between now and the end of this year.

- Whether your company can achieve any of these types of results is difficult to tell at this point in time. But one fact is certain: You are the one person who can take the action necessary to help us quickly determine what the possibilities are.

- You know your enterprise better than anyone. Would you welcome an effort to uncover similar or even greater results? Together we can quickly determine what, if any, possibilities exist.

- Since both of our companies are committed to [total quality management programs], it would be interesting to get together to see if we can use these principles to achieve similar or even greater savings in your area of [profit and loss].

- Do these results fit in your business plans for the balance of this [year]? You may be asking yourself; "Can these people actually deliver similar or greater results?" The fact is we don't know. However, with your guidance we can quickly find out.

You're almost there!

Take the time to create your ending paragraph in the space provided. I invite you to use any one of the examples shown previously as a starting point. All of the ending paragraphs you just read were taken from actual VITO correspondence that has proven to be enormously successful in getting to VITO.

Write your ending paragraph here:

_____

_____

_____

_____

_____

_____

_____

_____

_____

_____

_____

### PART FIVE OF THE FAB FIVE: YOUR CALL TO ACTION

Your call to action sits at the very bottom of your correspondence. It's the very last few sentences of your correspondence.

It is a powerhousepostscript (or P.S.).

In this postscript, you must always give VITO a choice of different ways that you or they can take action. There are three different ways to do that. Pick the one that suits you.

1. You state a day, date, and time that you're going to call VITO.
2. You give VITO two choices of days, dates, and times that they can call you.
3. You provide VITO with a "fax-back" form with questions that they must answer before either of the aforementioned two action items takes place.

*Do not* use any of the following options as part of your call to action:

1. Suggest a date for a face-to-face meeting. *Do not* write this in your postscript: *"I would like to set up a meeting on Wednesday at 10:00 so I can show you the many ways that our 'Cure-all' industrial cleaner can save your janitorial staff time and money."*
2. Suggest that VITO call you with any questions. *Do not* write

this in your postscript or in any other part of your letter: *"If you have any questions, call me at your earliest convenience."*

3. Make a nebulous suggestion that you contact VITO. *Do not* write this in your postscript: *"I'll call you some time next week to set up an appointment."*

These approaches will run your Equal Business Stature right into the highway divider.

Over the years I've tested and proven various ways to get VITO to respond favorably to my call to action and take my telephone call. What follows is the best of the best. Notice that in each case I use VITO's PA's name. In a later chapter we'll cover exactly how you get this precious information. For now, assume that you've mastered the get-the-personal-assistant's-name skill.

Example Number One:

*P.S. I'll be calling your office on Tuesday, May 14 at [9:00 AM]. If this is an inconvenient time, please have Tommie inform me as to when you would like for me to call.*

Example Number Two:

*P.S. I'll be calling your office on Tuesday, May 14 at [9:00 AM]. If this is an inconvenient time, you can call me on Friday, May 10 or Monday, May 13 between [3:00 and 5:00 PM].*

Or:

*P.S. I'll be calling your office on Tuesday, May 14 at [9:00 AM], or if you prefer a more convenient time, please let me know by calling my direct line: 800-777-VITO.*

Example Number Three, Fax-Back:

This one is my personal favorite. If you try it, it will be yours, too. It works like a charm!

*P.S. I'll be calling your office on Tuesday, May 14 at [9:00 AM], or if you prefer you can fax back the attached form.*

Create a form similar to the one you see in the following box. You'll be amazed at how well it will work.

# facsimile transmittal

| | |
|---|---|
| **FROM:** | **Mr. VITO Benefito** |
| **TO:** | **Tony Parinello** |
| **FAX TO:** | **1-800-777-VITO** |
| **DATE:** | **Tuesday, May 14** |

**MESSAGE:**
I would like for you to contact:
Name: _____
Title: _____
Telephone Number: _____
On one of the following dates:

       Choice #1:_____/_____ at: _____:_____ AM/PM
       Choice #2:_____/_____ at: _____:_____ AM/PM
       Choice #3:_____/_____ at: _____:_____ AM/PM

**Other Comments:** _____
_____
_____
_____
_____
_____
_____

A word or two about your closing salutation:

Not too long ago I received a correspondence from a high-net-worth financial planner here in San Diego. The letter was printed on elegant paper, and it addressed several of my areas of interest. It also stated that this firm paid close attention to all the many critical details that a professional financial planner takes pride in for a select clientele. All very impressive. However, I was shocked to see that the sender had neglected to sign the letter! Don't make that mistake. Sign your masterpiece!

Speaking of which, here are some suggestions for the words to use:

*All the best*

*To your continued success*

*Make today a masterpiece*

*To greater results*

*To a more predictable future*

*Here's to our future*

Don't use the closing salutation *"Sincerely yours."* Why? Webster's dictionary defines the word *sincere* as "not deceitful or hypocritical; honest and genuine." If you're really all of that, you don't need to say it. Besides, it's ho-hum and drab.

In closing this chapter I invite you to take a close look at the following sample VITO correspondence. Use it as your template. However, *don't use my words . . .* unless your plan is to sell *my* services! You can always get assistance in creating your correspondence to VITO by going to www.sellingtovito.com and joining Club VITO.

If you've completed all the exercises in this chapter *from VITO's perspective* (not yours), you should take a break and give yourself some kind of reward.

That's an order, private. You've just completed the core of this selling system. Congratulate yourself in some special way before you move on to the next chapter.

> *"65 of the Fortune 100 achieve up to 54% larger sales in one-half the amount of time using this man's ideas."*

May 11, 2004

Ms. Importanta
President

Dear Ms. Importanta,

The results stated above are common achievements for our business partners. As much as 50% of revenues previously wasted on unintentional inefficiencies are now channeled directly into increased shareholder value, an annuity stream that continues to provide ongoing benefits for everyone; except their competition.

We are pleased to present the following areas of proven repeatable achievements in the computer software industry but, more importantly: which one of these areas are you personally convinced that there is room for improvement between now and the end of this calendar year in your organization?

*Increased add-on business from existing customers* by as much as 120%. We agree it is amazing, but when your salespeople build unshakable loyalty at the top, add-on business goes up and the need to win back goes down.

*Reduced sales cycle times, while increasing Time to Readiness.* It's hard to argue with ideas that are proven to lower expenses while at the same time impact in a favorable way efficiencies of revenue generating employees.

*Increased efficiencies of knowledge workers.* Turn around time of sales critical documents is decreased as much as 23%. Now, every team member will consistently have the correct information when they need it.

Ms. Importanta, with your direction we can quickly determine if we can assist in providing equal or even greater results. Our personal promise to you is that if we cannot deliver our promises we will not ask for your business partnership.

To your greater success,

Will Prosper
858-777-8486

P.S. I will call your office Tuesday, May 14 at 9:00 a.m. If this is an inconvenient time, please have Tommie inform me as to when I should place the call.

# 15

---

# WAVE GOODBYE
# TO SEEMORE

---

**Proven VITO Principle #15: Conclusions *are* starting points *for* VITO.**

Let's take stock of what we know so far.

We know that VITOs *can* and Seemores *can't*.

We know that a substantial majority of VITOs were once sales-people and that virtually all of them know the importance of sales to the organization's future.

We know that VITO demands results and respects the individuals who can deliver them.

We know that VITOs are impatient.

We know that VITOs love to win and hate to lose anything.

We know that VITOs are always on the lookout for new ideas and that they know they don't know it all.

So—knowing what we know—how the heck do we approach these distinctive, highly productive egomaniacs? In short, all of this makes for great entertainment!

I've had the pleasure of interviewing some of our nation's great-est marketers on my Internet talk show. These are specialists in all types of marketing: print, direct mail, niche, Internet marketing, and everything in between. And although each had a unique idea about their craft, they all agreed on one particular tactical element:

If a person sees and/or experiences a product or idea a minimum of seven times, that person is then familiar with that item or concept and will then entertain the possibility of investing in that item or concept (assuming that they haven't disengaged from the approach).

No one seems to know the *real* reason why seven is the magic number, but everybody seems to agree that it's true. Now, I have personally met more salespeople than most individuals walking on this planet. I have also met more VITOs than most individuals walking on this planet. What I've learned is that both of those populations do not fall into what you or I would call *typical.* As a matter of fact, they are *atypical* and disposed to avoid just about any type of mainstream behavior and/or thinking.

Based on this fact, I have developed and proven a strategy for approaching VITO that delivers results that are repeatable.

In this chapter you'll discover what that process is. As you would expect, it is shorter than seven steps.

## WHAT YOU CAN EXPECT

If you've taken the time to do all of the exercises that I've detailed in prior chapters, what you're about to learn will change your career. You will become the master VITO salesperson you were born to be! You'll make so much money that you'll need a high-net-worth financial planner. You'll be able to buy every toy you've ever wanted and take incredible vacations in total style. Yes, you're about to become the salesperson of the year, if not the century—if you implement what follows.

On the other hand, if you *haven't* taken the time to do all of the exercises that I've detailed in prior chapters, what you're about to learn will make little to no sense to you. If you make any attempt to wing it and try it anyway without first doing your work, you will fail.

If you're ready to proceed, so am I.

## THE WAVE

Earlier, we spoke about the Fabulous Five parts and the nine correspondence elements that every correspondence to VITO must include.

> What we're about to do right now is create a *wave* of four relevant pieces of material for VITO that incorporate everything you've learned thus far. We're going to send these pieces to them *in advance* of our telephone call or in-person visit.

You will choose what four delivery modalities to use from the following list of correspondence assets:

1. First-class mail.
2. Postcards.
3. Faxes.
4. E-mails.
5. E-presentations.

You and I will put into action a marketing approach at a mere fraction of the cost that your company would normally spend to create the type of stir that will result from what you're about to learn and do. When it's all said and done, your VP of marketing will be very, very curious about what you've been up to. He or she will want to know exactly what you've done to pack your sales forecast to capacity with individuals (VITOs) and organizations who are *totally predisposed to buy from you.* Let's get started . . . shall we?

### THE POWER OF VITO FAMILIARITY

Picture VITO sitting in his or her office. It's quiet; VITO is deep in thought. VITO is searching for the one idea or solution that no one has yet presented to him or her. *Why* is VITO searching? Either or both of the following reasons:

1. VITO has a deep desire to win.
2. VITO must somehow grow shareholder value quickly and ethically.

VITO's PA has placed today's incoming mail on the desk, and as VITO takes the last gulp from that wheat-grass protein drink, VITO notices something. Sticking out from the pile is a bright crimson-colored postcard.

Curious, VITO grabs for it and reads its 30-word message:

> Your e-mail contains an idea from our CEO on how to grow shareholder value.
> The title is "My Call on Thursday, May 14 at 10:00 AM."
> We invite you to read it!

### What's Going to Happen?

VITO's behavior is going to be utterly predictable. VITO will either check the e-mail in-box for the titled message . . . or hit the intercom button and ask the PA to do it.

Either way, the e-mail isn't going to be there. It's too soon. But VITO, as we know, is impatient.

So VITO will leave the postcard out in plain view on the desk—or perhaps make a mental note or quickly key it into his or her PDA: *"Look for e-mail from CEO re: 5/14."* Alternatively, VITO will make sure that the PA is on the lookout for that e-mail.

Later that day, VITO gets the e-mail titled "My Call on Thursday, May 14 at 10:00 AM." And bless VITO's heart, VITO reads every single word of it.

### What Just Happened?

You just hit pay dirt in the world of getting to VITO by using one of the great forgotten tools in sales correspondence: a simple postcard with no more than 30 words on it.

Forget about printing them, forget about putting postage on them, forget about sorting them, and forget about having to design them. Just go to www.USPS.com—that stands for United States Postal Service, of course. Click on "direct mail services." Then click on "premium postcards" and bingo! You've landed in the point-and-click "create-my-best-ever-postcard" world of getting to VITO!

The postal service really will (virtually) help you design your postcard, print it out, and mail it that same day—first-class mail, for about 40 cents each—no matter how many or how few you send!

In the preceding getting-to-VITO scenario, I've used a postcard to alert VITO of an imminent e-mail and piqued VITO's interest.

Here's an example of some other uses for a VITO postcard:

1. Set a time for your first telephone call to VITO.
2. Alert VITO that an e-presentation is on its way to them (more on this in a few paragraphs).
3. Alert VITO that you'll be stopping in to see one of their line of business executives on a certain day, date, and time.
4. Invite VITO to an "executive telephone seminar" between you and your existing customers and, of course, a few prospect VITO accounts.
5. Take the place of a letter yet have all the contents of the letter. (You'll see an example of this in a just a second.)

Here's an example of a VITO postcard that works:

*"We booked 15 million in new business in just 6 months using one of this man's ideas."*

May 11, 2004

Mr. VITO Benefito, CEO

Dear Mr. Benefito,

Imagine the impact to your top, middle, and bottom line with similar or even greater results. It's great news for your stockholders. We've been able to provide the following results for over 65 of the Fortune 100.

Larger entry point orders to 54%

Shorter sales cycles by as much as 50%

Greater add-on business up to 120%

It's too early to tell if we can assist in the accomplishment of your strategic initiatives between now and the end of this quarter. But one issue is certain: You're the one person who can make the call to action to find out.

To greater results,

Anthony Parinello
800-777-VITO

P.S. I'll call your office on Tuesday, May 14th at 10:00 AM to discuss the many different possibilities. Or, if you would like, you can reach me Monday through Friday between 3:00 and 5:00 PM PDT.

## MY EDITORIAL ON VITO POSTCARDS

This postcard complies with all of the required elements of VITO correspondence we discussed in Chapters 13 and 14. (By the way, don't forget to send your signature to the USPS site electronically so your postcards are properly signed.)

## YOUR E-MAIL TO VITO

E-mail has been beaten into the ground. Even so, we can't seem to live without it.

I strongly advise you to never send an e-mail to VITO unless you send something in advance of your e-mail—like the VITO postcard we've discussed. (You can also send a VITO fax or a VITO letter, which we'll discuss in a moment.)

If you want to send an e-mail—and I suggest you do, just don't let it be the first thing you send—here are some tips:

1. Make sure that your e-mail follows the guidelines that we've already established for correspondence to VITO in Chapters 13 and 14.
2. Make sure you use a compelling topic or subject line. (My favorite is *"Our call on Thursday, May 14 at 10:00 AM"*).
3. Give VITO an audio option.
4. Give VITO a link to go to a particular page on your company web site.
5. Give VITO a link to your private or personal web site.
6. Give VITO a link to go to a web site that's personally branded to them. (Very cool.)
7. Include attachments for all of the line of business executives that you'll need access to in the initial stages of your sales process with VITO, Inc. These attachments must be included by name and by title and written in a way that VITO can easily understand.

You'll be able to see examples of each of these by going to www .gettingtovito.com and clicking on "Chapter 15 online assets."

Those are the dos. Here are the don'ts.

1. Don't use any language that VITO will not understand or connect with. This includes any product names, numbers, technobabble, industry jargon, buzzwords, and acronyms.
2. Don't forget to call at the prescribed time your call to action states. (Of course, this applies to all forms of correspondence that state that you'll be calling.) Make sure you take into account any time-zone difference that may exist between you and your prospect. (It only takes one stupid mistake to flush your credibility down the porcelain fixture.)
3. Don't pick a date and a time that's insensitive to VITO's business environment. For example, you may want to avoid the end of the month if your prospect is in the business of manufacturing anything.

Here's an example of a VITO e-mail that works:

**Date:** Friday, 10 May 2005 15:42:34 + 0700
**From:** "Tony Parinello" tony1@sellingtovito.com
**To:** vitoimportanta@vitoinc.com
**Subject:** Our telephone call on Tuesday, May 14 at 9:00 AM.

Dear Ms. Importanta,

Currently 65 of the Fortune 100 use my sales process to increase the size of each initial sale by as much as 54% while at the same time cutting their sales cycles nearly in half.

More importantly if you decide to embrace our unique ideas we suspect that we can deliver similar or even greater results to your entire sales team within the next 120 days.

Attached are specially prepared documents for three members on your executive staff:
Attachment A:    Jacob L. Wilson, Vice President of Sales
Attachment B:    Julia Smithsonian, Vice President of Marketing
Attachment C:    Bronson C. Davids, Vice President of Channel Markets

I invite you to forward all three informative and relevant documents so we can begin a dialog with the team members you trust the most to deliver greater sales performance.

I'll call your office on Tuesday, May 14 at [9:00 AM] to get your opinion of our future business relationship and what next step you would like to take. If this is not a convenient time you can select a more suitable time by clicking on www.TonyParinello@sellingtovito.com

If you would like you can view an executive overwiew of my ideas. Simply click on this link: www.msimportanta@stv.com

## MY EDITORIAL ON VITO E-MAILS

Notice that this e-mail has attachments arranged by name and by title for each of the individuals who normally would engage in the evaluation and decision-making process for your products, services, and solutions.

This is, as I have said, a key element of your e-mail to VITO. Notice also that the tie-in paragraph makes a direct request of VITO: *"Please forward the following attachments to . . . ."*

It doesn't matter whether VITO or VITO's PA opens and reads this e-mail . . . your request will not be forwarded to anyone at VITO, Inc. *without that initial recipient reading it first.* That means you just hit getting-to-VITO pay dirt!

Why? Because at that moment, VITO and/or their PA will have, right there on the screen, your entire value proposition for VITO, Inc., written in *VITO-ese*!

Please do make sure that each attachment is written clearly for VITO. Use words, phrases, and thoughts that VITO can easily understand and connect with. I know you've read these words before, but they are so very important, they really are worth repeating.

## E-PRESENTATIONS

Imagine for a moment that the postcard, letter, or fax you send to VITO has this brief message on it:

> Your e-mail contains an e-presentation with ideas on
> growing your shareholder value titled
> "My Call on Thursday, May 14 at 10:00 AM."
> My CEO invites you to watch it!

Now imagine that you created that presentation and sent it to VITO.

It's amazing how many tools are available in this area that aren't being used by salespeople. I've got two favorite authoring tools that you'll be able to experience by going to www.gettingtovito.com and clicking on "Chapter 15 online assets." They are both extremely easy to use and will merge your voice (or the voice of your CEO, or a satisfied VITO who is using your stuff) with your Microsoft PowerPoint slides.

As you assemble your e-presentation, consider the following points:

- Any e-presentation you create and send must be as short as possible.
- You must never exceed three slides per presentation.
- You must never have more than 20 words on each slide.
- You must never speak for more than 10 seconds per slide.

Also, don't show the names of your other customers unless:

- They are customers shared by you and this VITO
- They are prospects shared by you and this VITO
- They are suppliers of this VITO
- They are on this VITO's board of directors

Here's an example of an e-presentation: What you're about to see are my actual slides. The audio is contained in the online example waiting for you at www.gettingtovito.com. Of course, your presentation will be much different from mine.

Slide one:

*Increased Sales Revenue*
By as much as 54%
*Time-to-Revenue*
Cut by up to 50%

Slide two:

*Assets Required:*
Nine people
$870,000
5% risk
*Return on Investment:*
Six months
Up to 2,000%

Slide three:

*65 of the Fortune 100*
*Over 1.5 Million Salespeople*
*1,500 presentations*
*90,000 individuals each month*

## MY EDITORIAL ON VITO E-PRESENTATIONS

One of the best tactics that I've learned over the years about giving a presentation to VITO (as opposed to anyone else on the face of the earth) is that you should put the slide you would normally present as your last slide first . . . and proceed backward from there!

How did I learn this? By mistake! I'll never forget it. I was working for Hewlett Packard at the time. We were required to use the slide set provided by our corporate headquarters; it was about 30 slides too long. But that's what headquarters wanted, so that's what we did.

Except for the one presentation that I goofed up. I mistakenly put my last slide in first. That slide showed the ROI that VITO could expect.

When it came up on the screen, I was as surprised as my audience (which happened to be a large manufacturing company's president, CFO, and plant manager) when the CEO looked me square in the eyes and said "How confident are you that HP can deliver these results?"

Instinctively, I answered confidently: "100%."

The CEO stood up put his hand on the CFO's shoulder and said quietly to her: "Julia, make this happen." And then he left the room!

I shut off the projector and said, "What's the fastest way for us to accomplish what your CEO wants?"

I won that deal in record time. But more important, I learned an important principle about communicating with VITOs. Things the rest of us consider *conclusions* (like ROI) are *starting points* for VITO.

Put your last slide first and proceed backward. Forget all that other stuff about your company's history and the project parameters and everything else. For VITO that translates as "Yap, yap, yap . . . blah, blah, blah." Skip it.

*VITO doesn't care who you are until*
*VITO understands what you can do . . . for VITO.*

## FIRST-CLASS MAIL

These days e-mail is so popular that first-class mail is almost forgotten in some circles. All the more reason to send VITO a letter that conforms to the principles you mastered in Chapters 13 and 14. Let's review them, shall we?

1. *The Headline sits prominently at the top of the page.* There's no logo, just a plain piece of white paper; also notice the Headline is bold, italicized, and centered.

2. *The date is on the right-hand margin.* The date is on the right-hand margin because common business letters place dates on the left-hand margin. This letter to VITO is no common piece of mail, so we'll put it on the right.

3. *No inside address! VITOs know the name and address of the enterprise they built!* Inside-addressing a letter was needed half a century ago when automated mailing and sorting machines destroyed an envelope every now and then. The inside address provided a way for the post office to ensure delivery of the letter. That just doesn't happen any more. Remember VITO's need for recognition? Sure you do . . . the sweetest words any VITO will ever see and read—and the ones that should go at the top of any letter—are VITO's name and title!

4. *All paragraphs outside the Benefit Bullets are indented and are not fully justified.* Translation: Use hyphenated words; don't format it so the right side of the text is even. Here again, this is common letter-writing etiquette. Here again, this is no common letter!

5. *The Benefit Bullets sit in the middle and are prominently displayed.* The reason we make this area visually appealing is that it contains brief statements of our proven ability or areas of highly probable results that can take place if VITO takes your call to action. Look at it this way. If all VITO reads is the Benefit Bullets, you win!

6. *The ending paragraph is easy to see and read.* You'll recall that this part of the VITO letter introduces a level of uncertainty and in essence challenges VITO to take the first step. If VITO were only to read this paragraph, he or she would be drawn into the rest of the letter almost automatically.

7. *The Action P.S. is the last element and sits low on the page.* Reading habits indicate that once the Headline is read and does its job and the reader reaches a logical break point in the letter (like some white space), the reader's eyes are going to drop to the bottom of the page. If all VITO reads is the Headline and the Action P.S., you'll still be getting your message across powerfully.

Here's how you'll send it:

In a *plain white* envelope, no logo, no razzmatazz.

Use your own name and your company's address.

Drop the suite number.

Along the bottom of the envelope, on the flap side, write this: "Contains information for our telephone call on Thursday, May 14 at 10:00 AM."

Want to make it even more powerful? Sure you do. You may choose this version instead:

"[Tommie], this contains information for Ms. Importanta's call on Thursday, May 14 at 10:00 AM."

## MY EDITORIAL ON VITO LETTERS

They are powerful!
They get results!
I promise!

I challenge you to send no less than 50 letters to the VITOs in your sales territory. Follow up appropriately. You be the judge of whether they're worth your time and effort. If you don't get at least a 45% letter-to-conversation rate (on the phone or in person), something is very wrong. Check the format, check the language, and go back and reread Chapters 13 and 14.

A note of caution: These letters are specifically formatted for VITO. They simply won't work for anyone else. Trust me. Don't even try it!

The VITO letter breaks all of the rules in the book of how to write an "effective and proper" business letter. It does so intentionally.

Who, in every organization on earth, writes the rules? Who can change the rules when they want to? Who can break the rules if they darn well please?

You guessed it. VITO.

## FAXES

VITO faxes can and do work wonders. But don't use your standard, run-of-the-mill company-issue cover sheet. You know—the one that has your logo proudly displayed at the top of it . . . the one that has your 800 numbers and address on it . . . and so on. Instead, take a completely different approach:

Use an 8½″ × 11″ size copy of the envelope that you sent your letter in.

Where the postage would normally go, write the words *Please Hand Deliver.*

Sheet number two could, of course, be your VITO letter! Slightly modified, to include a few choice hand-written annotations, accompanied by arrows pointing to various areas of your VITO letter, such as:

- *An arrow pointing to the Action P.S.:* "looking forward to chatting with you!" (We'll get to that phone call in the next chapter.)
- *An arrow pointing to one of your Benefit Bullets:* "Do you consider these to be uncommon improvements?" or "Are you looking for similar or even greater results?"
- *An arrow pointing to the Headline:* "Is this an area of concern for your upcoming quarter?"

Sheet number two could also be your VITO postcard. VITOs love options, so why not give them one or two? Suppose you were to create an 8½″ × 11″ rendition of your postcard, informing VITO of the e-mail or e-presentation. Do you think that would get their attention? VITOs love this stuff!

Here's what it might look like:

---

*"My coach is the Nation's leading expert that's why I am 184% of quota!"*
David Wilson, Charleston, NC

Dear Mr. Benefito,

How many of your salespeople can make that statement? If you think there is room for improvement in any one of your salespeople's quota performance I invite you to go to:

# www.sellingtovito.com

Click on: Sales Leaders and discover what the VITO™ Sales Process can possibly do for your entire team.

*Tony*

Tony Parinello
Vice President of Sales
1-800-777-VITO

---

You could add a third sheet which could be a fax-back form. Here's what it might look like:

# facsimile transmittal

**FROM:**    **Mr. VITO Benefito**

**TO:**       **Tony Parinello**

**FAX TO:**   **1-800-777-VITO**

**DATE:**    **Tuesday, May 14**

**MESSAGE:**
I would like for you to contact:
Name: _____
Title: _____
Telephone Number: _____
On one of the following dates:
        Choice #1:_____/_____ at: _____:_____ AM/PM
        Choice #2:_____/_____ at: _____:_____ AM/PM
        Choice #3:_____/_____ at: _____:_____ AM/PM

**Other Comments:**

_____
_____
_____
_____
_____

### *Five Thoughts for Getting Even More Creative with Your VITO Fax*

Get a copy of VITO's annual report. Take the front page and use it as your cover sheet. Here are some ideas for what you could write on that unorthodox cover page:

- An interesting idea follows to assist in [accomplishing your mission]. See page two.

- See page two for our idea to [shorten time to revenue]. (*Note:* What you'll put in the brackets is the most talked-about initiative that you read about in VITO, Inc.'s annual report or what you know that they're interested in just by the nature of the industry they're in.)
- We have an early adopter idea for your consideration . . . see page two.
- See page two for the first of three steps to ensure [under-budget over plan] performance for your entire [sales team]. (*Note:* What's great about this approach is that it builds curiosity prior to your telephone or in-person follow-up . . . more on this in a later chapter!)
- [Increase knowledge-based worker effectiveness while lowering expenses.] See page two.

### YOUR WAVE: THE BLENDED APPROACH

In picking written communication modes, you might find yourself migrating toward what *you* feel most comfortable with. However, as I've already mentioned, *your* comfort zone isn't what's important here. What is at stake is finding out what will push one or all of VITO's buttons and put your products, services, and solutions in the best possible light *before* you pick up the phone.

Here's how I personally mix the approaches we just talked about. This sequence has worked very well for me. I invite you to give it the chance to produce incredible results in your own sales work.

#### *Wave Number One*

1. Send a first-class letter.
2. Pick up the telephone and call as per your Action P.S.

Or:

3. Make an in-person appearance at the time suggested in your Action P.S.

### *Wave Number Two*

1. Send a postcard.
2. Send an e-mail.
3. Pick up the telephone and call at the time suggested in your Action P.S.

### *Wave Number Three*

1. Send a postcard.
2. Send a unique, personalized e-presentation.
3. Pick up the telephone and call at the time suggested in your Action P.S.

Or:

4. Make an in-person appearance at the time suggested in your Action P.S.

### *Wave Number Four*

1. Pick up the telephone and call (talk live or leave a voice mail message).
2. Send a unique, personalized e-presentation.

### *Wave Number Five*

1. Send a fax.
2. Send a unique, personalized e-presentation.
3. Pick up the telephone and call at the time suggested in your Action P.S.

My guess is it's going to take a bit of trial and error on your part to figure out what's most appealing to the VITOs in your territory. If you have any concern about being in violation of any government regulation by using any one of the five combinations you just read, talk to your sales manager and get his or her approval. Don't forget to maintain an accurate "drop list" of people who ask not to receive further messages from you.

(Make sure that in every single case the prospect company to which you're sending your wave fits your TIP to a "T." See Appendix A.)

Unfortunately, I can't guarantee that you won't aggravate or agitate some VITO who happens, for whatever reason, to be having a horrific day. If you wind up pushing VITO's "irritation" button, use the following phrase, which has always worked well for me:

> "I am very sorry that my approach was not received in the way it was intended.
>
>     Ms. Importanta, what would you like for me to do?"

Now that you know the right sequence for *approaching* VITO . . . what do you actually say during the conversation?

Read on!

Don't forget to go to www.gettingtovito.com for additional for-free and for-fee information!

# Part Three

---

# BEST PRACTICES

Welcome to Part 3! In this part of the book we'll examine all of the best practices for getting to VITO. The question now is whether you are ready to pick up the telephone and make the call to VITO, taking advantage of what is *proven to work*. If your answer is Yes, then let's proceed.

If you're having some last-minute concerns about picking up the phone or showing up in person at VITO's doorstep, then before you move into this part of the book, quickly flip to Appendix B and meet my personal success coach, Steve Dailey. Steve has helped me over the past years to accomplish the most powerful steps in my life and my sales career. He can help you too.

# 16

---

# THE VOICE
# OF POWER

---

**Proven VITO Principle #16: When VITO speaks,
others listen.**

---

Power has a voice, and VITO uses it. You can, too. In this chapter you
will begin to learn how to speak—not talk, but speak—to VITO.

Before we *look* at the principles for success when it comes to
speaking to VITO, let's *listen* for a moment . . . to the voice of a
VITO.

Whenever you listen to a VITO, you'll hear a certain tone, modulation, volume, and pace. I want to suggest that your own voice is
equally rich and equally capable of that confident delivery. I'm not
suggesting that you mimic, model, mirror, or make any other lame attempt to sound like VITO. What I want you to sound like is *yourself,*
just like VITOs sound like the most confident version of themselves.
I want you to sound like the confident, self-assured salesperson that
you really are.

## THE TONE OF YOUR VOICE

Have you ever had the experience of listening to your voice on a
recorder or on your own voice mail? Have you ever said to yourself,
"Boy, I hate the way my voice sounds"?

If so, you're not alone. The majority of the population has the same response of dislike to their own voices. Why do you think that is? I think it's because most of us don't use the natural tone of our voice when we speak and because, thanks to the makeup of our inner ears, we hear a different tone in our own ears than others hear.

The tone you use in interacting with VITO will determine how easy (or difficult) it will be for VITO to process your message. The natural, and most appealing, tone of your voice is actually the tone of your "hum."

This probably isn't the vocal tone you habitually use during conversations. But it should be!

If you want to find and use your natural voice, simply practice a little each day by picking your favorite song and humming a bar . . . then singing that same bar. Pick the same song for several days in a row, then change the song. In next to no time, your natural voice will appear effortlessly in all of your conversations, whether on the telephone or in other situations.

## MODULATION

How well do you use your voice to express emotion?

If you've been spending most of your time selling to Seemores, chances are you've had the experience of walking away from a conversation or in-person visit not really knowing whether or not Seemore was excited about your ideas. That's because most Seemores don't emote!

When you're in their presence, you most likely find yourself holding back a bit . . . not wanting to overpower them.

It's time for a change!

Most every VITO I've interacted with over the years has emoted well and vividly with his or her voice. You won't hear a sing-song type of presentation from a VITO, with plenty of mindless highs and lows. What works best for the person who emotes (like you) is a vocal modulation *appropriate to the topic and emotions of the discussion at hand.* Not everything we say is as appropriate as everything else. When something is particularly important, or when you're asking VITO a question, the way you modulate your voice should change. If you're looking for guidance on this score, close your eyes and listen to one of the nightly network news anchors deliver their text. If you're *still* not familiar with what I'm talking about here, just listen carefully to Oprah Winfrey as she interviews someone, and you'll know *exactly* what this paragraph is talking about.

> Generally speaking, you'll want to raise the pitch of your voice during the last few words when asking that thought-provoking question . . . and lower the pitch of your voice during the last few words when you're making a powerful statement of fact to VITO.
>     *This takes practice. Invest the time and effort necessary to get it right.*

Again, keep this in mind: When VITOs speak, people listen. That's because they speak with the other person's purpose in mind. If there's one master rule for effective vocal communication with VITOs, it's understanding what VITO's purpose is and subtly using your voice to emphasize what's relevant to that purpose.

## DON'T TURN UP THE VOLUME

We learned a simple principle when we were children: The more important your point is, the louder your voice should be. Unfortunately, when you're speaking to VITO this is a big mistake!

In a professional setting your volume should remain *totally* constant, period. Judicious use of *silence,* or modulation of tone or pitch, is the best way to emphasize any point you want to make to VITO.

## PACING

Pacing is the speed at which you speak. It *must* match the speaking speed of VITO. No exceptions.

The higher up in the hierarchy you go, the less time you have to make your point. I always plan the pace of my monologue to suit the person and his or her regional culture. Let me mention here that the world-class sales trainers I've met over the years are in profound disagreement when it comes to agreeing upon how much time salespeople have before the person on the other end of the phone loses interest and disengages from the call (either mentally or physically). My estimate is that you and I have a meager eight seconds, whether speaking on the phone or in person, to get to the point and get a reaction.

That may seem like a very short time, but try this experiment: The next time you're driving and you stop at a red light, when the light turns green, *wait eight seconds* before you hit the accelerator. After you reach *one thousand and four,* you'll hear lots of horns and yelling voices. When you get to *one thousand and six,* you'll have a few fingers lifted at you. By the time you reach *one thousand and eight,* you may well feel a nudge on your back bumper!

Eight seconds is a very long time indeed!

## TWO POWERFUL POINTS TO PONDER ABOUT THE SPOKEN WORD

### *Point Number One: Urgency*

The element of time is deeply interwoven into each and every reward that VITO hopes to achieve at VITO, Inc. Time is *the* critical factor, and that means urgency counts. You must clearly articulate how time intensifies the achievement of any specific goal, plan, objective, strategic initiative, or reward.

Before you make your first telephone call or show up for your first appointment with VITO, I urge you to calculate your estimate of the total time-to-value of your ideal products, services, and solutions for this VITO. Get specific. What time frame have your other customers experienced in realizing results? If you don't have any customers, what's your forecasted best estimate? Once you know this you need only to find out what *this* VITO wants to accomplish and *when* this VITO must take action.

You can accomplish this by asking a question along these lines:

*"Mr. Bigshot, so we can serve your specific needs, what's personally important to you about [moving your operations to southern Florida] between [now] and the [end of this fiscal year]?"*

Notice the use of the word *personally.* This will encourage VITO to *emote* the "what" for you. The incorporation of the concept of time adds the element of urgency and will give you an idea of the "when."

### *Point Number Two: Curiosity*

I've yet to meet a VITO who wasn't extremely curious. Do everything you possibly can to raise the level of VITO's curiosity, whether it is in your correspondence, over the telephone, within a voice mail message, or during in-person meetings.

Remember—in your communications, you must use ethical, compelling, and curiosity-building phrases like:

> *"There's much more to discuss that I would prefer to go over in person."*

VITO thinks: "What is it she wants to tell me in person?"

During your scheduled telephone conversation with VITO, you could mention right up front that before the end of the call you'll want to disclose an important benefit to him or her for the overaccomplishment of a certain goal, plan, or objective.

Use phrases like:

> *"Please remind me to cover . . ."*

Or:

> *"Before we end our call we'll talk about one powerful idea to . . ."*

During your first in-person appointment with VITO, use something very similar to the following phrases. These phrases must *replace* the typical icebreaker we've all been taught to use. Remember, icebreakers are for ships, not salespeople!

> *"In just a moment we can explore what [65 of the Fortune 100] . . ."*

> *"Before too long, let's make sure we talk about . . ."*

> *"Before the end of our time together . . ."*

## BEFORE YOU GET TO VITO BY TELEPHONE

I've learned the following insights from my own experiences in telephone conversations with VITO. I invite you to factor them into your interactions.

1. *Never follow a script or try to commit anything to memory.* Let's face it. A conversation with VITO is stressful. Yet if the call turns into a "what does my script say" exercise, you'll lock up, get cotton mouth, stress out, and sound awfully stupid—like some lonely, behind-quota telemarketer. VITO will disengage instantly. Accept that you must improvise, and don't be shy about telling VITO something like this: *"You pose an interesting question. Let me give it some thought. Is it acceptable to you if I get the answer by two this afternoon?"* So here's the point: *Say you don't know what you don't know . . . and internalize your message rather than attempting to memorize it.* Speak from your gut, not your head. Be sure you sound natural and totally unscripted. Your opening monologue should never sound the same way twice. This will keep it interesting for you and, more important, for VITO.

2. *Be authentic.* Don't try to be someone else. Be yourself. May I suggest a mantra:

*"Today, I will be the best me that I can be."*

3. *Reinforce your Equal Business Stature by presenting a balanced-gain equation.* Balanced-gain equations express the *entire* picture of value that you can offer VITO, Inc. They show the up side *and* any down side of your ideas. Some balanced-gain equations may have no down-side risk; just the same, the equation must always be balanced. You *must not* sound like a robot reciting text, of course. Keep in mind that VITOs are whole-brain thinkers. Half stories don't add up in their minds. For example: *"We've got a proven track record with three other [high net-worth financial planners] for increasing [returns while minimizing all risks]."*

4. *Never ask VITO, "Did you get my letter?" or any variation thereof.* Everyone hates this, and VITOs have a special loathing for being interrogated about administrative details like whether they've received a piece of paper in the mail. Not a great way to build Equal Business Stature! No one is likely to appreciate the implication that they're delinquent in opening, reading, or paying attention to incoming mail. If you sent a letter, e-mail, e-presentation, fax, or whatever, simply repeat one or two of the points you raised in it, and from that point on let VITO connect the dots. As an aside, whenever you say to VITO "Did you get my letter?" you may be reminding them

that they're at the preliminary stages of a memory retention problem. Ouch!

5. *Relate your expert industry knowledge.* Your products, services, and solutions have the potential to change VITO, Inc.'s enterprise-wide performance. If they didn't, you wouldn't be bothering to reach out to VITO. Your first job is to relate relevant accomplishments and experience to VITO. But don't drone on! Remember, you're operating under an eight-second time limit. Identify the *highlights* of your company's best experiences with customers.

6. *Provide a choice of several ideas.* VITO, more than any other individual in the enterprise, requires choices. VITOs often give commands that sound like this: "Find me the top three producers of compressed air injection molds for our project X—and do it fast!" Get used to saying something like this: *"The three most powerful ideas we have for your consideration are increasing the size of every entry point order from new customers, cutting sales process time in half, and getting more high-margin add-on business from your existing customers. Which of these is most important to you between now and, let's say, the end of this fiscal quarter?"*

7. *Near the end of your first conversation, suggest action items.* This is particularly important when talking to VITO. The trick is, you have to do this in a way that allows VITO to give the orders. They love that! What you say might sound something like this: *"What would you like to see me and my team accomplish between now and the end of this business [day]?"* or *"Who on your team do you want me to continue this conversation with between now and the end of this business day?"* Once you've asked this question, listen up and take your marching orders!

8. *Don't be afraid to do a reality check!* VITOs, you'll recall, hate wasting time. They also *respect* anyone who hates wasting time as much as they do! That means that you can and should ask VITO for a kind of help that you can't ask of anyone else in the organization. It sounds something like this: *"May I ask you for a personal favor?"* VITO will say something like *"What's on your mind?"* What comes next can take you in several different directions . . . it all depends upon what you want. Remember, VITO isn't afraid to answer the tough questions. Here's what yours might sound like:

*"If you were me, would you spend the next six months selling my [ideas/solutions/results] to VITO, Inc.?"*

Or:

*"If I were your best salesperson, how would you personally coach me to sell to you and VITO, Inc.?"*

Ask these types of questions from anyone else in the organization and you won't get a straight answer. Ask VITO, and you'll get the straight scoop.

9. *Nervous? Say so!* In this point-and-click world, everyone, *including VITO,* is looking for closer, more-personalized business relationships. VITO wants to talk to real people . . . so why not be real? If you're freaked out that you've got a VITO on the line, why not say so? Try this: *"Just thinking about speaking with the CEO of the ABC company has made me a nervous wreck."* Don't be surprised if VITO responds with something like this: *"Yeah, I get pretty nervous when I've got to call my chairman of the board . . . what's on your mind?"*

10. *Keep the door open.* Before you say goodbye at the end of your first conversation, say something like this: *"I'll keep you posted as I meet your other mission-critical team members and uncover their needs."* Don't ask this: *"Would you like for me to keep you posted on my progress?"*

Now you're ready to get to VITO and follow your wave into their world. In the next chapter, you'll examine the specific elements of your phone conversation with the top banana. Chapter 17 . . . and VITO . . . is waiting for you on the next page!

# 17

---

# SIX GOALS
# FOR THE BIG
# PHONE CALL

> **Proven VITO Principle #17: Speak what's on VITO's mind, and VITO will listen!**

There are six goals of your Big Phone Call to VITO. (I'm specifying the initial phone call because it's a common initial point of contact, but the truth is that the six goals that follow are universal goals that will apply to each and every verbal interaction you have with VITO, particularly the first.)

The goals are:

1. Making a great first impression.
2. Making whatever you say sound conversational.
3. Speaking with unshakable confidence.
4. Connecting what you say to what you sent.
5. Establish what's happening next.
6. Making a great last impression.

Let's look at these goals one at a time, shall we?

## GOAL #1: MAKING A GREAT FIRST (AND LAST) IMPRESSION

You've heard it a million times: "You only get one chance to make a first impression." True enough, and first impressions are certainly important, but I've come to see that the *last* impression is really the one that VITOs seem to remember. It's what you say as you close the call and/or walk out the door that's most remembered.

With this critical fact in mind, let's understand that our goal is going to be making a *memorable impression* . . . not having our impression become a distant memory!

*Give VITO an idea that they will only get from you.* Imagine VITO sitting in his or her office. The phone rings, and VITO answers. (I know, I know; that's not a given. We'll talk about voice mail in a later chapter.) VITO hears the voice of someone he or she has not yet met (you) confidently offering an idea that VITO didn't think of. You're somebody in the know with new, fresh ideas. (How do you *get* these ideas? You get them from your customers and/or your own VITO, that's how. You get them from reading trade magazines and joining and participating in associations that pertain to the industry you're calling on. In other words, you get them from being interested, showing up, and taking a risk.)

*An alternate approach: Ask VITO a question that no one else will ask.* VITO is sitting by the phone. It rings. VITO answers and hears a very smart-sounding salesperson (you) asking a question that makes VITO think . . . a question that challenges VITO in a good, sound business way . . . a question that makes VITO think or say out loud: *"That's a great question!"*

Consider incorporating the following kinds of questions into your first conversations with VITO:

- What's important to you personally about _____?
- Tell me more about _____.
- Could you be more specific about _____?
- If you could change one aspect of _____, what would it be?
- What proof do you need to see (or hear) that would interest you enough to take a closer look at _____?

- What are your top three goals for _____
  between now and (some period of time)?
- What's the biggest problem you're having in _____?
- What improvements would you like to see in _____?
- Could you give me your opinion on _____?

Whether you open the conversation by sharing an idea or asking a question, be sure you *articulate whatever you say to VITO using words and phrases VITO can easily identify with and understand.*

This is very important! Perhaps the fastest way to end a conversation with VITO is to use words and phrases that are unfamiliar to him or her. No one likes to feel uninformed . . . and VITOs hate it. Using strange words and phrases is a challenge to VITO's ego, power, control, and authority. Not a good strategy. Don't do it.

### A Word or Two about Icebreakers

"How are you today?"

"Did you get that frost down at your place last night?"

"Is this a good time?"

"Do you have a few minutes?"

Icebreakers are for ships, not salespeople! They waste precious time, and they don't help you out in establishing Equal Business Stature. Skip 'em.

In the old days, icebreakers were supposedly used to reduce tension in a typical initial- contact situation. Here's my question: Who's tense, anyway? VITO sure isn't. Icebreakers are awkward, self-serving, inappropriate, and insulting. I'm not kidding. Don't use them, either on the phone or in person. Start right in with something that matters to VITO.

My good friend and fellow sales trainer, Dan Sideman, collects icebreakers. Here's my favorite from his collection:

As the young salesperson walks into the prospect's office, he gives a quick glance at the picture on the prospect's credenza. In an attempt to show off his attention to detail, make a great first impression, and reduce tension, the rep uses what sounds like a classic icebreaker.

"Wow!" he says. "How did you manage to get your picture taken with John Madden?"

"That's not John Madden," the prospect replies. "That's my wife!"

End of appointment. End of sale.

Here's another true icebreaker story. I pick up the phone to call the CEO of one of the largest manufacturing companies in the world. Much to my surprise, the CEO himself answers his own line (yes, it really does happen) and says the three words for which I am utterly unprepared:

"This is Sam."

I respond with a lame attempt to break the ice and build rapport: "What a surprise, I expected your assistant."

"Hold on," VITO says instantly. "I'll get her for you."

Click. Sound of phone ringing. Sound of assistant's voice mail message. That's one golden opportunity, gone forever. It seems like I'll never stop making mistakes! That's how I learn the best, though . . . how about you?

## GOAL #2: MAKING WHATEVER YOU SAY SOUND TRULY CONVERSATIONAL

The fastest, easiest, and most reliable way for me to teach you how to keep your first exchange conversational is to suggest that you make a regular habit of reviewing the principles you read in Goal #1 and then keep current with developments in your company and your industry, looking constantly for new topics of conversation that you feel comfortable discussing with VITO. Then set yourself apart from and above everyone else by raising your ideas and asking your questions . . . and watching what happens!

By the end of this chapter you'll have plenty of new ideas to use for your telephone and in-person approach to VITO. Then you'll internalize that approach. Once you internalize it—not word for word, but concept for concept, idea for idea—you'll throw away whatever notes you used to create it and never look at or listen to them again. When you call your prospects you'll never, ever make your pitch the same way twice. You'll be authentic in your approach.

That means you won't be perfect. You won't even strive for perfection. Sometimes you'll make mistakes. You won't take yourself too seriously when things go well or when things go poorly. You'll be able to relax, smile, and yes, even chuckle a bit.

When you think about it, getting good at placing calls to VITO is a lot like getting good at being a human being.

### *Be Willing to Laugh!*

Recent research shows that children laugh on average 400 times each day. The average adult, on the other hand, posts 15 laughs per day.

I can't prove it with statistics, but my gut tells me that VITOs laugh more often than anyone else in their organization. You should, too.

## GOAL #3: SPEAKING WITH UNSHAKABLE CONFIDENCE

Confidence—or faith, if you prefer—is the opposite of fear. Confidence is how super VITOs and super salespeople (like you and me) consistently respond favorably to the inevitable challenges with our marketplace, quota, and growth goals, and product shortcomings. It's how superstars respond to the competitive and business pressures that come their way on a daily basis.

Confidence is a way of thinking and doing. Confidence is probably the single best way to create success when you're up against a real challenge.

There are strategies that will help us in our quest to become unshakably confident in our business and personal lives. Just go on line and search on the word *confidence* and see what you get. A plethora of books, assessments, audio programs, coaching programs, online courses, confidence camps, eco-trips with guest speakers on building confidence. They're all there!

I've mentioned this in a previous chapter, and it's important, so I'll say it again: When all is said and done, your brain and its power can just as easily work against you as in your favor when it comes to using all of these confidence-developing tools. The reason: your brain, my brain, VITO's brain, *does not know the difference between a negative and a positive phrase.* It just takes the command and processes it, however it's delivered.

So, for example, if you think "I don't want to blow this VITO call" your brain (and mine too) hears: "Blow this VITO call!"

But if you think "I'll make this a massively successful VITO call!" your brain (and thankfully mine too) hears: "Successful VITO call!"

Here's a great confidence-building ritual related to our VITO sales work on the phone. After every VITO call you make, write down *at least one part of the call that went well.*

For example:

1. Got past receptionist gatekeeper
2. Built rapport with VITO's PA
3. Got VITO's voice mail direct dial number

Next, write down *only one part* of the call that you'd like to improve the next time around. For example:

1. Leave a shorter, more direct voice mail message

You might just as easily have written "put greater power in my voice," "take a shunt more proactively," or "thank whoever I speak to for their time."

Here again, notice that the item that you want to improve upon is written in a positive statement. Our tendency would be to write statements like these:

- "My voice mail message is too long."
- "My voice is too weak."
- "I took the shunt too soon."
- "I didn't say thank you."

What kind of programming is that? Notice the profound difference between how the brain will process these two messages:

*Put greater power in my voice.*
versus
*My voice is too weak.*

Let's not beat ourselves up, OK? Instead, let's visualize positive change—and command our minds with positive statements. The act of visualizing and thinking positive change, constantly, throughout the day, is a consistent habit of successful VITOs and superior salespeople. Make it your habit too!

## GOAL #4: CONNECTING WHAT YOU SAY TO WHAT YOU SENT

The best way to create an environment of success when it comes to getting to VITO is to follow the "wave" right into VITO's office. (See Chapter 15.) When you follow this type of process, your call to VITO will be expected on VITO's end and on your end. You'll feel more purposeful during your telephone or in-person approach. You're still putting the blueprint together, I know, but for now think about the following four principles of connection:

1. You will, as a general rule, be sent directly to the person you sound the most like. Therefore, when you connect the dots, make sure you sound like the person you happen to be talking to—that is, VITO.
2. Speak in shorter rather than longer sound bites, making sure that each and every phrase you say is a complete thought.
3. When referencing anything that you sent in your wave, use terms like these: "as you know," "as you're aware of," "in materials you've already seen," and "a process you're already knowledgeable about." (Notice how different these phrases are from "Did you get my postcard?")
4. Always have everything that you sent in your wave right in front of you when you make the call. Leave nothing to your memory. Write brief "bullet points" and key questions on your copy of what was sent, and check them off as you get to them.

## GOAL #5: ESTABLISHING WHAT'S HAPPENING NEXT

Let's face it: At some point during the process of getting to VITO you'll be shunted to someone that VITO trusts to take charge of the tactical steps necessary to do whatever it is you're speaking to VITO about. My personal goal when I am making my VITO calls is to *suggest* the shunt with a statement that sounds something like this:

ME: "Ms. Importanta, who on your staff would you like for me to continue this conversation with between now and the end of this business day?"

VITO will always give me the name of that certain someone I should continue with. However, if I want to make sure that the conversation with VITO continues and still give VITO a way out so he or she can continue with what is no doubt a busy day, I can say something like this:

> ME: "Ms. Importanta, who on your staff do you trust the most to continue this important conversation with me between now and the end of this business day?"

Here's what's interesting. Whenever I add the words *"trust the most,"* VITO will always respond with something pretty darn close to "Let's just take the time to cover it now."

What does that mean? Perhaps, just perhaps, VITOs don't trust anyone as much as they trust themselves!

Try the question, and you can come to your own conclusions. All I can tell you is that VITO's behavior when I pose the question is utterly predictable.

## GOAL #6: MAKING A GREAT LAST IMPRESSION

You really have *two* chances to make an impression: at the beginning of your interaction with VITO and at the end of it. One of the fastest ways to make a great last impression is say something pretty darn close to this near the end of your telephone or in-person conversation:

> *"Mr. Benefito, when we meet [the next time we get together] I'd love to hear the story about how you started your company."*

Or:

> *"Ms. Importanta, when you find the time I'd love to understand what your specific vision is for _____."*

Or:

> *"Mr. Bigtime, if you could find the time I'd love for you to tell me how you select your business advisors."*

Don't be a bit surprised if VITO says to you, "Why wait? Let's do it now."

You should budget time for this kind of discussion. Be sure you've planned about 30 to 45 minutes for each of your VITO interactions. You'll find that once VITOs get started, they find it hard to stop!

## PUTTING IT ALL TOGETHER

You can implement all six of the ideas you just read about if you follow one simple rule: *Think like an entrepreneur, think like VITO!*

If you're selling for an organization that has a VITO (my guess would be it does) and he or she thinks like an entrepreneur (my guess is he or she does) and you happen to be selling your products, services, and solutions to organizations in your sales territory that are run by VITOs (they are) who think like entrepreneurs (they do) . . . then guess what?

You as a salesperson must learn to adopt an entrepreneurial mind-set. What does that mean? Let me answer that question by posing these questions for you before we go on to the next chapter. (Any response along the lines of "What has this got to do with selling?" means you may not really be ready to implement the ideas you've been reading about in this book.)

1. Do you know how many customers your organization has?
2. Do you know what your organization's profit margins are?
3. Do you know what your cost of sales is?
4. Do you know what your cost of goods sold is?
5. Do you know what your organization's strategic initiatives are?
6. Do you know who's on your board of directors?
7. Do you know who's on your board of advisors?
8. Do you know what college or university your own VITO went to?
9. Do you know what philanthropic organizations your VITO is involved with?
10. Can you articulate with a fairly high degree of accuracy what your organization's marketing plans are?

11. Can you articulate with a fairly high degree of accuracy what your organization's customer service or care plans are?
12. Can you articulate with a fairly high degree of accuracy what your organization's supply chain looks like?

You may want to get the answers to all of these questions before you send your wave and make your call to VITO.

# 18

---

# THE VITO "ELEVATOR PITCH"

**Proven VITO Principle #18: What you say is what you get.**

Let's set the stage. You're picking up the telephone to make the call to VITO. For right now, assume that VITO *will* pick up the phone; when you follow your wave into VITO's office 10 to 20% of the time VITO will in fact pick up his or her own phone totally unprotected!

So suppose that takes place. What the heck do you do?

Read on to learn what goes into a great "elevator pitch" for VITO.

### THE TYPICAL SCENARIO

Usually, when VITO picks up the phone, you hear VITO's name:

"This is Sally."

or

"Sam Bigdeal."

Or, if you happen to be calling a VITO in New Jersey, VITO might just say:

"It's VITO—whaddya want?"

(One thing I truly love about the old "hood"—it really hasn't changed much over the years!)

---

## YOUR FIRST STEP

Repeat VITO's name. Keep things formal—use Mr. or Ms., for example:

VITO: "This is Sally."

You: "Ms. Importanta?"

VITO: "Yes."

This approach does not conflict with building Equal Business Stature and making a great first impression. It's just a matter of showing respect for someone you haven't yet had a chance to meet in person and get to know. If VITO says his or her entire name, you *should not* repeat it! Instead, you'll use their entire title and company name:

VITO: "This is Sally Importanta."

You: "The CEO of ABC Manufacturing?"

VITO: "Yes, that's me."

At this moment, you have VITO's undivided attention. Whatever she was doing prior to your saying her name, she's now stopped doing. Whatever that was . . . signing checks, shaking hands, patting backs, giving high-fives, scaring babies . . . doesn't matter! VITO is now paying attention and is waiting to hear what you will say next.

Be very careful! What you say next will make *all* the difference in the relationship and delivering a stellar elevator pitch.

What most salespeople do now—despite ample and endlessly repeated warnings not to—is say something like this:

"Hi, Ms. Jones. This is Will Perish, with the ABC Insurance Company. Is this a good time?"

Now, unless your name is, say, Tony Soprano or your company affiliation is, say, the IRS, I can tell you what's going to happen next. VITO will respond to your self-defeating verbal hara-kiri by giving you the gift of a dial tone.

Or tuning you out.

Or asking you to send written information.

Or repeating the phrase "I'm not interested" slowly and purpose-fully.

Or asking briskly: "What's this about?"

*None of these reactions will help you implement what you've learned so far in this book.*

## WHAT TO DO INSTEAD

What I am going to tell you now is probably in direct conflict with what you've been taught for years. I don't care. Do it anyway.

When VITO says "Yes" or "Yes, this is Sally" or "Go ahead," you're going to respond with something confident, positive and enthusiastic, something that *does not directly identify you, your company, or the ideas you eventually want to discuss with VITO.* Instead, you're going to use a simple "Pleasantry."

## THE PLEASANTRY

Take a look at the Pleasantry in action.

VITO: "Yes."

You: "What a pleasant surprise. It's great to finally speak with you!"

or

You: "Thanks for picking up the phone!"

You: "Thanks for taking my call."

You: "It's an honor to speak with you."

You: "It great to speak with the person who'll appreciate the following idea . . ."

You: "You're just the person who'll appreciate this idea . . ."

Don't get all freaked out if VITO responds to your Pleasantry with "Who is this?" If that happens you can respond with something along the following lines:

You: "Sorry, forgot to tell you. this is Will, Will Prosper with Julia Designs of Colorado right here in Fort Collins."

Then, without any hesitation, move quickly and sure-footedly to . . .

## THE HOOK, GRABBER, UNIQUE SELLING PROPOSITION (USP), BULLET, SIZZLE—OR WHATEVER ELSE YOU WANT TO CALL IT

Immediately after your Pleasantry, you're going to keep VITO's attention by saying something that's linked directly to something that you revealed somewhere in the most recent part of your wave. Here's what it might sound like.

### Example #1

You: "One of our ideas has increased revenues by as much as 4% while cutting expenses up to 12% in three months for six of the top ten manufacturing organizations here in San Diego."

### Example #2

You: "One of our ideas has substantially increased revenues while dramatically cutting expenses in just three months for six of the top ten manufacturing organizations here in Lodi."

Did you notice the difference between the two examples above? The first one uses percentages, and the second one uses descriptive words. Which one is better? Good question!

Here's the answer: Neither. It's been my personal experience they both work great!

### Example #3

You: "Finding and resolving unintentional inefficiencies in [sales operations] is an area that we've become experts in. One example is increasing return on sales while maintaining current budget levels for the coming year."

Make sure that somewhere in your grabber you mention an item of intense interest to VITO. In my example, it's sales operations (that's a pretty safe bet).

*Warning:* Never, ever ask obvious, stupid questions that will insult

VITO's intelligence, such as "Can you tell me a little bit about your operation?"

Other important points to bear in mind:

- VITOs are whole-brain thinkers; as a result, you must present whole ideas.
- Go easy on the success stories and name dropping. Generally speaking, relative ranking name-drops work best: "three of the top ten . . ." "four of the biggest . . ." "two other CEOs in your industry. . . ." Of course, if you know for a fact that your potential name-drop is on VITO's board of directors, is a customer of VITO, or is a major, critical supplier to VITO, Inc., you should definitely use that name.
- Remember—give VITO choices whenever possible. "There are two particular areas we can offer ideas in: ensuring compliance to recent government regulations and resolving unintentional inefficiencies in [sales operations]. . . ."
- Don't try to press for an appointment. VITO doesn't really like it.
- Stay away from any variety of technobabble. This, for instance, won't work: "We can investigate the probability of providing three different levels of interchangeability at the component, subassembly, and unit level. Which one is most important to you between now and the end of your current project?"

### What Your Hook Should Do

Your hook is the heart of what you say on the phone at the beginning of the conversation. It should be:

1. Rich in results.
2. Stated with what I call a balanced gain-equation. (I'll tackle this in a minute.)
3. Time focused.
4. Rooted in social proof.
5. Capable of establishing credibility and Equal Business Stature—and, by extension, capable of positioning you as VITO's thought partner.

Let's look at each of these in depth.

*Important Hook Ingredient #1: Rich in Results*

There are two categories of results that just about every product, service, and solution ever created can deliver: tangible and intangible. We've talked about this briefly; recall that tangible results or hard-dollar value is easy to see and/or measure and should be expressed using numbers and/or percentages, whereas intangible results or soft-dollar value cannot be measured definitively, may involve emotions or perceptions, and should be expressed using descriptive words and/or phrases.

*Important Hook Ingredient #2: A Balanced Gain-Equation*

Like everyone here on planet earth, VITO is motivated by one of two desires:

1. The desire to achieve a rewarding experience.
2. The desire to avoid a painful experience.

That's it. Simple, isn't it?

"Yeah, Tony . . . sounds great. But what the heck is a balanced gain-equation?"

Okay, here at last is the scoop on this critical VITO selling concept. By showing the up side *and* the down side of your idea, you can appeal to *both desires!*

By doing so, it's a safe bet that you'll make your point relevant to the entire population of VITOs in your sales territory: VITOs who are motivated by the desire to experience pleasure *and* VITOs who are motivated by the desire to avoid pain.

Take another look at one of the statements I gave you earlier. Notice that it *balances* both the securing of pleasure and the avoidance of pain.

> You: "One of our ideas has *increased revenues* by as much as 4% while *cutting expenses* up to 12% in three months for six of the top ten manufacturing organizations here in San Diego."

In other words, you focus not *just* on how you increased revenues (getting a gain) but how you did so *while cutting expenses* (eliminating a pain).

*Important Hook Ingredient #3: Time*
Everything in VITO's world revolves around time. When you make a statement of your ideas, capabilities, products, services and/or solutions you must include the element of time. Specify the period of time it will likely take for *this* VITO to realize similar or even greater results.

*Important Hook Ingredient #4: Social Proof*
Generally speaking, VITOs fall into the category of "early adopters." They're not afraid to play pioneer and take a few arrows in the process . . . as long as there are rewards throughout the journey. Even so, you should play it safe by introducing what I call *social proof* in your hook. This will help you establish credibility early on.

1. Verbalize a direct quote from a happy existing customer: "Ima Bigshot at Stellar Products increased her new product revenue by as much as 12% while cutting up to 53% off their time-to-market in just nine months." Here again, only use Ima's name if you know the following:
   • Ima is not a direct competitor of VITO, Inc., *and/or*
   • Ima is a customer of VITO's board of directors or board of advisors, a customer of VITO, Inc.; or a supplier to VITO, Inc.
2. Use a direct quote from the leader or line of business executive in your organization: "Our CEO is inviting you to find out how we may be able to help increase your new product revenue by as much as 12% while compressing your time-to-market by up to 53% in as little as nine months. That's why you're hearing from me today!"
3. Play it totally safe and use a "relative ranking" name drop: "One of our ideas has increased revenues by as much as 4% while cutting expenses up to 12% in three months for six of the top ten manufacturing organizations here in San Diego."

I'm emphasizing these points—which I know you've read before—because they are critically important to the task of getting to VITO.

*Important Hook Ingredient #5: Credibility, Equal Business Stature, and Your Position as VITO's Thought Partner*

This one is easy! If you do everything else I've laid out in this chapter, exactly as I've laid it out, you will win credibility and Equal Business Stature. As far as being VITO's thought partner, you'll earn this position by hitting a bull's-eye in any one of VITO's areas of interest.

And how do you know what's important to VITO? Ask! Don't ask VITO. Ask someone that VITO knows quite well. Who's that? VITO's private assistant, that's who!

Here's how it works. You pick up the telephone and specifically ask the receptionist gatekeeper for Ms. Importanta's private assistant. Here's what happens next.

> TOMMIE: "Ms. Importanta's office, Tommie speaking. How may I help you?"

> YOU: "Tommie, thanks for taking my call. This is Will Prosper with Jacob Consultants. May I ask a personal favor of you?"

> TOMMIE: (in a rather suspicious and somewhat standoffish voice): "What's on your mind, Will?"

> YOU: "Which one of the following three strategic initiatives are *you and Ms. Importanta* most eager to achieve between today and the end of this [week, month, quarter, half, year]: [shorter time to market, lowering of expenses, full compliance with strict governmental regulations]?"

Of course, all the words and phrases in brackets should be tailored to this VITO.

Don't be a bit surprised if Tommie tells you exactly what you're looking for. (Isn't that what sales is all about—asking?) And don't be a bit surprised if you call fully expecting to talk to Tommie and wind up speaking to VITO because Tommie is away from the office. That's exactly why you've got to be totally ready to speak to VITO at any time.

## GETTING INTERRUPTED

Now, before we proceed to the next part of our elevator pitch, let me warn you about something. At the very moment in time when you start to articulate your hook, something extraordinary might just happen. You may get interrupted by VITO.

Not to worry—this is a beautiful thing! If your hook is doing its job, VITO is indeed very likely to cut in and say something like the following:

"This sounds familiar . . . did you send me a letter about this?"

or

"This sounds interesting—tell me all about it."

or

"I think I read something about this just recently."

or

"This sounds vaguely interesting."

or maybe even

"I have absolutely no interest." (Click . . . dial tone. I hate it when that happens, but sometimes it does. Let's get over it!)

Whatever interruption you get, stop right where you are and pay rapt attention to what VITO is saying. For all intents and purposes your monologue is officially done and the all-important dialogue is about to begin.

## WHAT'S YOUR NAME?

If you don't get interrupted and you've articulated your hook, VITO knows the reason for your call. The cat's out of the bag. *This* is the perfect time to identify yourself—not beforehand. If you'd like, you can also identify your organization. If you choose to identify your employer, say a little bit about what makes your organization as great as it is. Remember, though, that whatever you say has to fit into one brief sentence. It should sound pretty darn close to this:

You: "This is Will, Will Prosper, with Jacob Consulting—the hardest-working company in the outsourcing industry today."

## THE END OF YOUR ELEVATOR PITCH

You're going to conclude your elevator pitch with an ending question that incorporates some element of time. This should run no longer than two sentences. Check out these examples.

You: "Ms. Bigshot, does this touch on issues that are of concern to you this [month/year/quarter]?"

You: "Is this something you'd like to explore further?"

You: "What are your thoughts right now?"

You: "Have I touched on an issue that affects your day-to-day operations?"

You: "Who besides yourself would you like for me to talk to about our ideas before the end of this business day?"

You: "Who on your team would you like for me to continue this important conversation with between now and the end of this business day?"

### *Yes, That Last One Asks for a Shunt. Here's Why . . .*

VITOs will always take the opportunity to tell you where to go, who to see, and what to do. They spend all day long doing that anyway. And they love doing it. So, with this in mind, consider giving VITO the opportunity to shunt you. Then say:

You: "Mr. Benefito, before anyone else in your organization spends their valuable time with me, let me ask you . . . can you see any reason you would not financially support a decision to use my organization as one of your business partners between now and, let's say, the end of this [quarter]?"

Don't say another word. What you hear next will reveal exactly how much opportunity there is for you at VITO, Inc.

## LET'S PUT IT ALL TOGETHER

Here's an example of an elevator pitch that's worked well for me. Of course, yours shouldn't sound *exactly* like mine, but it should be about this long, and it should incorporate all of the elements you've read about in this chapter.

Remember, our goal is to *win interest and attention,* typically by eliciting some significant comment or interruption. And remember, this discussion follows the written wave we discussed in Chapter 15.

VITO: "This is VITO."

ME: "Mr. Benefito, it's great to finally speak with you! By the way, sixty-five of the Fortune 100 are increasing the size of each and every sale while at the time cutting their cost of sales in half. The real surprise is that we were able to help them do this in just ninety days! Oh, sorry, forgot to introduce myself: Tony, Tony Parinello with VITO Selling. Mr. Benefito, who on your team would you like for me to continue this important conversation with between now and the end of this business day?"

Diagram it:

| | |
|---|---|
| VITO's name: | *Mr. Benefito,* |
| Pleasantry: | *it's great to finally speak with you!* |
| Hook: | *By the way . . . sixty-five of the Fortune 100 are increasing the size of each and every sale while at the time cutting their cost of sales in half. The real surprise is that we were able to help them do this in just ninety days!* |
| My name: | *Oh, sorry, forgot to introduce myself: Tony, Tony Parinello with Sales Broadcasting.* |
| Ending question: | *Mr. Benefito, who on your team would you like for me to continue this important conversation with between now and the end of this business day?* |

Now you do it: Build your own elevator pitch here.

_____

I know this is a huge step in the process. That's why you may want to consider taking a moment to visit www.gettingtovito.com and click on "Chapter 18 online assets" for additional for-free and for-fee help.

After you've done that, we can move on to the next chapter, on the keepers of the key.

# 19

---

# ALLIES AT
# THE GATE

Mastering the skills necessary to create allies in and around VITO's executive suite is critical to getting to VITO. In this chapter we'll uncover the truth about how gatekeepers really feel about salespeople . . . then we'll dive into the world of the receptionist or gatekeeper.

How did I come across all this information about VITO's personal assistant? I interviewed a fistful of them in preparation for writing this book. What I found out was painful, but necessary, to hear.

What every salesperson on earth has to understand is pretty simple: Gatekeepers are God. Here's why:

*Do right by the Gatekeeper and you'll get right into sales heaven, that lovely place where really big sales happen really fast.*

*Do wrong by the Gatekeeper and you'll wind up in sales hell, that crappy place where really tiny sales happen really slowly.*

We must never, ever lie to God.

The common complaint I heard from personal assistants (PAs) and executive assistants (EAs) was that salespeople lied. That's how they felt in 1994, and it's how they feel today.

Maybe you're saying, "I've never lied to a gatekeeper." Great! Give yourself a pat on the back. For the rest of us it's time to pay the piper—and adopt a new way of building trust, rapport, and respect with the one person who has the power to keep you out or let you in.

During my most recent interviews I heard several specific complaints about salespeople from the gatekeeper, whom I call "Tommie." When you see the word *gatekeeper,* think of the smart, totally professional, utterly dedicated individual who serves with honor alongside the VITOs of the world.

Here are the six complaints.

## COMPLAINT #1: SCREWING UP VITO'S OR TOMMIE'S NAME

Talk about self-sabotage. Messing up VITO's name makes you a no-doubt-about-it master of disaster. Typically, salespeople don't take the time to pronounce the gatekeeper's name correctly, either.

*The setup:* Salespeople ask, "How do you pronounce B-e-t-s-e-y?"

*The rub:* After the salesperson is told "it's Betsey," the salesperson doesn't use the name again or says it incorrectly again—which is really dumb.

*The consequence:* The gatekeeper thinks the salesperson either has a learning disability or just doesn't care. The latter is most often the case, and the gatekeeper knows it.

*The remedy:* Before you wind up on VITO's doorstep, take the time to find out how the gatekeeper pronounces his or her name and how VITO pronounces his or her name. Ask the gatekeeper receptionist, *and write down the pronunciation . . .* or you could call a line of business executive in the same organization *and write down the pronunciation . . .* or you could call the top salesperson in the organization *and write down the pronunciation.*

## COMPLAINT #2: DIGGING FOR INFORMATION WITHOUT GIVING ANY INFORMATION

Like we work for the Department of Homeland Security or something. It drives Tommie crazy, and it doesn't help our cause.

*The setup:* Without announcing who they are, salespeople start asking questions like "Is VITO in?" or demanding, "Let me talk to VITO."

*The rub:* Guess what? No competent VITO gatekeeper will let anyone through to VITO without first figuring out who's calling and why they are calling.

*The consequence:* Gatekeepers would lose their high-profile, high-paying job if they complied with a stupid demand like "Let me talk to VITO" from a total stranger. The salesperson making such a ridiculous demand loses all credibility and is from that point forward treated like a child who's about to receive the equivalent of getting grounded for a week or having computer privileges taken away.

*The remedy:* This one is easy. When the gatekeeper picks up the phone and says, "Good morning, this is Tommie . . . how can I help you?" you say something that's pretty darn close to this: "Good morning to you! This is Bruce Brilliant from Lauren Designs . . . [Now swing right into your hook.]." Of course, if you've followed the process that I've been explaining for you throughout the book, you have sent a wave of correspondence that precedes your call. When you say your name, Tommie will most likely recognize it.

## COMPLAINT #3: BEING A JERK

Salespeople translate this as "not taking No for an answer," which sounds vaguely praiseworthy. Make no mistake. To Tommie, it translates as being a jerk.

*The setup:* Salespeople will ask a question, and if they get a No, they'll continue to ask the same question framed a bit differently. For example: "Is VITO in?" No. "When will VITO return?" I'M NOT SURE. "Would it be later on this morning?" IT'S HARD TO TELL. "Can I leave a message?" No. "Does VITO have voice mail?" YES. "Would you please connect me to it?" No—IT'S FULL, AND I'M THE ONE WHO CHECKS IT ANYWAY. "Okay, could you take my name and number?" No. MR. BENEFITO DOESN'T TALK TO SALESPEOPLE. GOODBYE.

*The rub:* This kind of exchange irritates the hell out of the gatekeeper, and it is quite common! It's so common, in fact, that the gatekeeper's patience level is basically nil. When a professional individual such as a gatekeeper experiences this, he or she will toast you and any idea you may have . . . even if it's a great one!

*The consequence:* You will not, ever, never get to VITO while this gatekeeper is on watch. You'll have a better chance at getting to VITO at a ball game or out in the parking lot. That's called stalking, though, so you can't do it.

*The remedy:* When Tommie picks up the telephone, say, "This is Jay Betterthantherest from Jacob, Smith, and Reasons—thanks for picking up. We've got an idea for you and Ms. Importanta to consider. What's the best way to . . ."

## COMPLAINT #4: NOT GIVING A STRAIGHT ANSWER

Gatekeepers believe that most salespeople are evasive and will not give a direct answer when asked a simple question. You know what? They're right.

*The setup:* (It usually goes like this.) Good afternoon, Ms. Importanta's office, this is Tommie. *"Is VITO in?"* No, who's calling? *"My firm has an important message for VITO."* What's the topic? *"It's an issue that concerns VITO about a strategic initiative that she's pursuing."* Okay, if you tell me the area you're calling about, maybe I'll be able to direct you to the correct resource in our organization. *"It might be better if I discuss this directly with VITO."* Tell you what, give me your name and number and I'll have someone call you back. *"It's Ima Gerk with Neveronquota, Inc. My toll-free number is 800-IMA-GERK. Should I repeat it, or do you have it?"* Nope, got it just fine.

*The rub:* Tommie hangs up, *never having written anything down.*

*The consequence:* If Ima ever gets up enough courage to call back, Tommie will open fire the moment she remembers Ima's previous call. Go ahead . . . make my day!

*The remedy:* Drag the folder of old tactics over to your metaphorical computer's "trash" and hit "empty." Your new skill set goes something like this:

Good afternoon, Ms. Importanta's office, this is Tommie. *"This is Will Winner with Gratebusiness. Tommie, we've got an idea for your consideration. If you think it's a good one, would you be willing to share it with Mr. Benefito at your earliest opportunity?"*

## COMPLAINT #5: LYING

If you just thought "Busted," even for a hundredth of a second, you have to change your approach to Tommie.

*The setup:* "VITO will recognize my name." "I met VITO at a chamber of commerce meeting last week." "I work out of your Boston office." These are common, shameless lies typically used by salespeople talking to Tommie. That last one was used by a salesperson attempting to reach a CEO of a Fortune 500 organization. Only one problem: The company didn't have a Boston office!

*The rub:* VITO's PA or EA already knows everything, everyone, and every place that VITO deals with. Lying is pointless.

*The consequence:* Any salesperson who lies to the Tommies of the world runs the risk of spending the rest of his or her sales career in sales hell. Remember: Never lie to God!

*The remedy:* Try this: Good morning, Ms. Importanta's office, Tommie speaking. *"Thanks for picking up! This is Will Prosper with Winner Technologies. We've never met or had the opportunity to speak. What do you think about . . ."*

## COMPLAINT #6: SLOPPINESS

Gatekeepers have come to believe that most salespeople are sloppy. Here's why.

*The setup:* Always in a rush, Louie Lastminute includes information he suspects may be unverified or outdated . . . but sends the letter anyway. He's busy.

*The rub:* The information is in fact wrong. Tommie sees this as a direct insult to VITO's place in the organization, especially when the error is something like, you know, VITO's title.

*The consequence:* Whatever Louie put together for VITO goes directly and immediately into the trash. Not fair? Think again. Tommie is paid to pay attention to details. Louie ignored them. If Tommie passes this letter along, that is basically the same thing as Tommie saying "Please don't give me a raise at my next salary review."

*The remedy:* Pretty obvious. Pay attention to every last detail of your written correspondence. When in doubt, have someone else check it out—as long as that someone else isn't a salesperson!

## OTHER ALL-PURPOSE REMEDIES YOU MAY WANT TO CONSIDER

File the following statements under "Things I Should Be Ready to Say to Tommie."

- *"We've taken the time to look at your web site, and I personally placed an order. I represent a company that specializes in stream-lining time-to-revenue. Are you the best person to share my ideas with?"*
- *"This is Ima Winner with Miki Davin Productions. It sounds like you're pretty busy. (Now wait for a long time. If Tommie doesn't say a word, continue:) Would you like to hear an idea that we've come up with as a result of purchasing one of your products from your web site?"*

When you're shunted by either Tommie or VITO:

- *Tommie, before you transfer me, could you tell me a little bit about Beth Roberts, your VP of marketing?*
- *VITO, could you tell me why you feel that your [VP of marketing] is a good fit for what we've got to offer your organization?*
- *Tommie, would it be OK if I mentioned your name to your VP of marketing?*
- *VITO, if your VP of marketing isn't interested, may I return to you for your [coaching/advice/suggestions]?*

## YOUR IDEAL DIALOGUE WITH TOMMIE

Tommie: "Ms. Importanta's office, this is Tommie."

You: "What a surprise—so glad you picked up. Are you look-ing for a fresh idea to increase your current revenue per trans-action while at the same time reducing expenses?

Tommie: "Who is this?"

You: "Sorry, there's so much excitement buzzing around this office about what we've been able to do to help other web-enabled companies, forgot to tell you . . . it's Ima, Ima Winner here at Miki Davin Productions. Let's see . . . where was I? Oh, yeah. Would you like to know more about my ideas?"

TOMMIE: "Well actually, VITO did say he was concerned about sagging revenue from our web initiatives."

YOU: "Hmm. That's fascinating. Could you share with me some of your concerns, Tommie?"

TOMMIE: "I can tell you this, VITO wants us to double our current revenues, and people are panicking over it."

YOU: "When would you like to see that result, Tommie?"

TOMMIE: "VITO says he wants to see something he can measure by the beginning of third quarter."

YOU: "Does it look promising for you to make that stretch goal, Tommie?"

TOMMIE: "VITO's concerned that we're off to a slow start."

YOU: "Tommie, let me ask you something else . . ."

See what's happening here? You are addressing Tommie directly with questions. However, Tommie is answering for VITO!

*Here's the rule: Ask in Tommie . . . receive in VITO!*

### TWO MORE GOOD TOMMIE IDEAS

- Write Tommie a nice thank-you note, but send it to VITO. When VITO opens it, she or he will walk over to Tommie's desk and hand-deliver it.

The next time you call Tommie, you'll get the royal treatment. Sales heaven just got three steps closer!

- Leave VITO a short voice mail message that sounds something like this: "VITO, your personal assistant Tommie and I had a very worthwhile conversation. She felt so sure that your organization could benefit from our ideas that she referred me to your vice president of marketing. I've initiated a call to her, and I'll keep you posted on our progress. Just one question before I let you go . . . if your VP really likes what she sees and is convinced that we can be of assistance, do you see any reason you would not support their decision to become a customer of ours? Oh, by the way, this is Ima Winner right here at Miki Davin Productions. You can reach me Monday, Wednesday, or Friday between 3 and 6 p.m. at 800-777-8486. Thanks for listening, and have a great rest of the day!"

You just took a typical interaction with VITO's personal assistant and created a not-so-typical interaction with VITO's voice mail. You informed VITO of your presence with the VP, you took a bold step and asked for VITO's support, you initiated Equal Business Stature, you qualified VITO at a high level, and (last but not least) you made Tommie look great! You did all of this with one single voice mail. Take a bow.

### A Brief Word about Receptionist Gatekeepers

Let's not forget the folks at the front desk (or whatever passes for a front desk in the twenty-first century).

They are the front line of any organization's "defense." They are tasked with making sure calls are routed to the best possible person. Contrary to popular opinion, their goal is not to make your life an everlasting existence in sales hell.

The easiest way to win over gatekeeper receptionists and get connected to VITO is to say who is calling before they ask—and, if need be, tell them exactly what the call is about before they ask. It's the old "head 'em off at the pass" technique.

Yes, that contradicts just about everything you and I have ever learned about getting over, around, past, under, and through these individuals. Ignore all of that stuff. Here's what the conversation should sound like.

Receptionist gatekeeper: "Good Morning, Jackson Supplies, how may I direct your call?"

You: "Would you please connect me with VITO Benefito? It's Will Prosper, thank you."

(Saying VITO's entire name and then saying your name sounds more conversational and informed. Always say the words "Thank you" at the end of your request, or just say the single word "Thanks.")

If the receptionist gatekeeper should ask "What's the call about?" all you have to do is deliver a slightly compressed version of a portion of your elevator pitch.

RECEPTIONIST GATEKEEPER: "What's the call about?"

You: "An idea that Mr. Benefito can use that can provide revenue gains while cutting expenses, which we've accomplished for another CEO. Would you please connect me? Thank you!"

Your call will go through if and only if you sound like the person you're asking to be connected to! In other words, if you want to speak to VITO, you'll need to *sound* like VITO.

What if you're asked: "Would you like to leave a message?" Keep reading!

# 20

---

# THE ART OF THE
# VOICE MAIL
# MESSAGE

Voice mail is one of the most powerful tools you can use in getting to VITO. But here's the rub.

The rule that I like to use for my voice mail messages is simple. I treat each and every message like it's a person-to-person interaction with VITO. That means that I must take my sales process with VITO one step closer to a win. When I do this, I feel that voice mail *is* a win . . . so I get excited when I get dumped into it rather than feeling it's less than a live conversation or less than what I wanted.

I have actually been hired to train entire sales teams to leave voice mail messages based on that principle. They liked the results. You will too . . . if you take to heart the advice that follows.

## SOME STATISTICS

As you know, I conduct VITO "Blitz" days for many of my Fortune 500 clients. During these powerful events, sales teams throughout a region or nation, send a wave to a target list of VITOs, and follow up with a phone call just like the one you've been reading about. Imagine several hundred calls to VITO being made in one single day!

Based on those calling days, I can say with confidence that if you follow my system you can expect the following things to happen.

- 10 to 20% of the time VITO will pick up his or her own phone totally unprotected by the gatekeeper(s). That's a significantly higher number than most salespeople would expect.
- The balance of the calling time is split 50/50.
  - 50% of the time you'll get voice mail.
  - 50% of the time you'll get Tommie live, which is a great outcome, too. (See Chapter 19.)

## WHAT TO DO

Remember, VITOs love processes—and they love individuals who follow them. Use this fact to your advantage. Set up a process.

On the day that you'll be making your call to VITO, if you should happen to get routed to voice mail you're going to deliver the best voice mail message that VITO will listen to that day. If VITO doesn't find the time to call you back, *don't get discouraged!* You're going to leave a second voice mail message *exactly* one week to the day and time from your first message, *and* you'll follow this process of one week to the day and time for seven full weeks.

Yep, you'll be leaving a total of seven messages. What will happen if you get to the seventh message without ever connecting to VITO? Well, in all of the years that I've been getting to VITO, after leaving literally hundreds of voice mail messages, that's happened to me so few times that I could count them all on one hand. So let's not even worry about that for now. I'll cover it at the end of this chapter.

## CALLING RULES

Once you send out a piece of correspondence that references a date and time for a call, you must make the call.

Once you leave a voice mail message you must leave another.

If you cannot follow up as you promised, if you cannot follow the process, if you stop short of completing the cycle, VITO will not be impressed. VITO will only do business with individuals who are as dedicated to their cause as VITO is to his or hers.

### WHAT YOU'LL SAY

Your first voice mail message could in fact be what you were going to say to VITO had she or he personally answered your call, with the addition of what I'll call "bookends."

In the voice mail example you're about to read, the bookends are italicized, and what I was going to say to VITO if I got VITO live is not italicized, and is taken directly from the Hook and Ending Question of my elevator pitch.

### *My Voice Mail Message #1*

*"Ms. Importanta, this is Tony Parinello. If you had been in your office to take my call, this is what you would've heard . . .* 65 of the Fortune 100 are increasing the size of every initial sale by as much as 54% while at the same time cutting sales process time up to one half! Ms. Importanta, are you looking for any improvements in these two sales performance areas in your organization between now and the end of this quarter? *Oh, wait a minute, this is voice mail and you can't answer that. However, you can reach me directly with your answer between 3 and 6 p.m. today, Wednesday, or Thursday of this week at 800-777-8486. Thanks for listening, and have a great rest of the day!"*

### *Write Your Message Text for Your Voice Mail Message #1*

Use the previous model to build a voice mail message of your own. Include relevant elements from the Hook and Ending Question of your elevator pitch.

_____

_____

_____

_____

_____

_____

### *Wait a Full Week for a Callback*

Don't get discouraged if VITO doesn't return the call immediately. Maintain your sense of purpose, and in one week, to the exact day and date of your first voice mail message, call again and leave your second message. Mine sounds like this.

### *My Voice Mail Message #2*

"*Ms. Importanta, this is Tony Parinello. Since my first voice mail message something very interesting has happened. Another CEO in your industry posted two stats that you may find interesting. I'll share one with you now and save the other one for our first conversation. Anyway . . . she increased add-on business from existing customers by 120%! Ms. Importanta, are you getting all of the high-margin business you deserve from your best customers, or do you think there is room for improvement? If so, I invite you to call me between 3 and 6 p.m. today, Wednesday, or Thursday of this week, or let me know of a good time to reach you. Here's my number: 800-777-8486. Thanks for listening, and have a great rest of the day!*"

### *Write Your Message Text for Your Voice Mail Message #2*

Use the previous model to build a voice mail message of your own.

_____

_____

_____

_____

_____

Another week of silence? Honor your process. Take a deep breath and call one week to the day and time from your last voice mail message. Here's my third message.

### *My Voice Mail Message #3*

"*Ms. Importanta, this is Tony Parinello. I haven't heard back from you, and I consider that a good sign. You're busy meeting deadlines and goals. The question really becomes . . . can my process and team of sales performance experts help you overachieve any of your critical goals? We're not going to be able to answer that question without you or someone you trust in your organization taking the first steps and finding out. You can call me between 3 and 6 p.m. today, Wednesday, or Thursday of this week, or let me know of a good time to reach you. Here's my number: 800-777-8486. Thanks for listening, and have a great rest of the day!"*

### Write Your Message Text for Your Voice Mail Message #3

Use the foregoing model to build a voice mail message of your own.

_____

_____

_____

_____

_____

_____

Yet another week of silence! I love a challenge, don't you?

You'll notice in my first three voice mail messages I presented ideas for moving *toward* goals and rewards: bigger sales, shorter sales cycles, greater add-on business, salespeople who are unstoppable, and so on. And you'll also recall that VITO has yet to return my call. So at this point, I figure maybe . . . just maybe . . . I've been leaving voice mail messages for a VITO who is more focused on trying to avoid fear, demise, doom, and disaster!

No problem. My next voice mail message will present what I call "consequence selling"—it's all about what will, can, or might happen if VITO *doesn't* have the benefit of my products, services, and solutions. Take a look:

### My Voice Mail Message #4

*"Ms. Importanta, this is Tony Parinello, with three questions that could change the course of your cost of sales. How much time do you think is being wasted by your sales team as they pursue their quota? Do you think that they are losing sales to your competition because they're not*

*getting to the approver of the sale? Worse yet, have they lost one single installed account this year? There is no reason for you to lose anything to anyone anymore. We have the answer to these and other problematic areas of the sales process. I invite you to take a moment and forward this message to the person you trust the most and have empowered to immediately stop losses from occurring in your sales process. I am here and available to take your call between 3 and 6 p.m. today, Wednesday, or Thursday of this week, or let me know of a good time to reach you. My number is 800-777-8486. Thanks for listening, and have a great rest of the day!"*

### *Write Your Message Text for Your Voice Mail Message #4*

Use the previous model to build a voice mail message of your own.

_____

_____

_____

_____

_____

_____

### *Double Up*

If I don't get a call back from my fourth voice mail message I might combine my message with a FAX or e-mail or e-presentation. I'll stay on the fear side of the motivation equation. In that case, my fifth message might sound like this. Here again, I'll leave this message one week later on the exact day of the week and time of my previous message.

### *My Voice Mail Message #5*

*"Ms. Importanta, this is Tony Parinello. I know how important your time is and that you're most likely in the very near future going to want to take the next step and get a better feel for what we can and can't do to stop the unintentional inefficiencies in your sales process. On your FAX machine is a study of a similar-size enterprise and the fact that they were losing 14% of their hard-earned customer base annually. In their*

*case it was costing them 1.9 billion dollars annually! We stopped it, and we can calculate exactly what your numbers are if you complete page two of the FAX, which is a short questionnaire. As always, the best time to reach me is between 3 and 6 p.m. today, Wednesday, or Thursday of this week. My number is 800-777-8486. Thanks for listening, and have a great rest of the day!"*

### Write Your Message Text for Your Voice Mail Message #5

Use the previous model to build a voice mail message of your own.

_____

_____

_____

_____

_____

_____

### Messages #6 and #7

These are usually highly customized to the situation of the VITO I'm trying to reach. I think of them as improvisation challenges. What else could I design that might connect with *this* VITO, in *this* industry, at *this* point in time?

Use those sixth and seventh messages, if they're even necessary, as exercises in personal creativity and customization. Adapt the principles you've learned in this chapter to the task of crafting special messages for special situations: Keep VITO's purpose in mind! Never use any language that VITO would not use. Never present an idea that VITO would not connect with.

Don't be afraid to use a little humor on the sixth or seventh messages; don't be afraid to leave a creative short message. Here's one of my favorite variations.

*"Ms. Importanta—this is Tony Parinello. You probably recognize my voice by now. Every night before I go to bed I talk to God. Why can't I talk to you?"*

Persistence really does pay off. Keep calling once a week, every week, for seven weeks, until you reach VITO. In the vast majority of cases, you will.

### What Happens if You Never Get a Call Back?

You have three choices.

First choice: Leave the following voice mail message.

*"Ms. Importanta, this is Tony Parinello. By my count you've received seven voice mail messages from me, and I've not received any return calls from you or anyone in your organization taking me up on my offer to uncover and resolve any unintentional inefficiencies in your sales process. That being the case, I'll plan on taking your enterprise off my prospect list for now, and I'll plan on contacting you [at the end of the third quarter] in the mean time. As always, the best time to reach me is between 3 and 6 p.m. today, Wednesday, or Thursday of this week. My number is 800-777-8486. Thanks for listening, and here's to your continued success!"*

Put this prospect in your CRM system as a wake-up call, and when your alarm goes off you can either send a wave (see Chapter 15) or just pick up the phone and give VITO a call.

Second choice: Send another wave. Change the Headline and the Benefit Bullets of your correspondence, and relaunch the entire process all over again.

Third choice: If your sales territory has plenty of possible suspects or prospects that fit your TIP (see Appendix A), file this one under the "tough nuts to crack" category and move on.

Before you proceed to the final pages of this book, take a minute and visit www.gettingtovito.com and click on this chapter's online assets for additional for-free and for-fee content.

# 21

## TEN STEPS TO VITO'S OFFICE

> **Proven VITO Principle #21: Learn to hate your competition.**

If you got here as the result of completing all the work that led up to this chapter, congratulations. You're ready to put the entire system into practice.

If you dropped in on this chapter without experiencing the exercises that preceded the page you're reading now, well, you're not *exactly* ready for prime time, but don't sweat it too much. Hey, I would have done the same thing you just did. After all, you're a salesperson . . . shortcuts are something like a way of life! I'm on your side; I am a salesperson just like you are. For your convenience, I've put the relevant page numbers that connect with each of the ten steps. In other words, I've left bread crumbs for you to follow. These page numbers will point you to the precise words in the body of this book that will help you *fast-track* your getting to VITO, sort of a VITO express. (If you landed here by reading through from the beginning, you're a trouper, and you may, of course, use these page numbers as tools for reviewing and reinforcing critical information.)

You'll notice that in each of the ten steps there are "mini" steps. Do them all. I've coached many different salespeople to perform the ten steps that you're about to take. The shortest time it took to put the process into effect was one day . . . the longest was three months. Not too bad a payoff considering the results that await. Bigger deals in less time . . . much bigger commission checks . . . selling large and living large . . . but there's a catch.

*You have to do everything laid out here, as it's laid out.*

### GETTING-TO-VITO STEP #1: CREATE YOUR TIP

Even if your territory has been split seven ways from Sunday; even if the rep before you and the rep before her and the rep before her didn't make quota, you will make—heck, exceed—your quota if you get to each of the VITOs in your sales territory who is predisposed to buy whatever it is you happen to be selling.

### *Do This*

1. Go to Appendix A (page 229) and complete your TIP.
2. Go to pages 97–116 and get your VITO-to-VITO referrals.
3. Move as quickly as you can to Getting-to-VITO step #2!

***Getting-to-VITO secret:***
When VITOs make sales calls, they only call on organizations that are predisposed to buy from them.

Stop wasting your time. Don't deploy any of what you learn in this book on prospects that don't fit your TIP to a "T."

### GETTING-TO-VITO STEP #2: ESTABLISH YOUR VALUE AND VALUES

VITO will only listen to value statements that relate to her or his world and only when such value statements are articulated in a way that VITO can easily understand.

If our business values are substantially different from VITO's, VITO will not support the efforts of anyone of a lesser authority within VITO, Inc. to find ways to do business with us. Therefore, we need to understand which of our business values will appeal to VITO.

### *Do This*

1. Go to pages 25–41 and read each and every paragraph that starts with a subtitle that has the words *value* or *values* in it.

2. Go to www.gettingtovito.com and click on Chapter 3 online assets and complete the value and values exercises. Make sure you do this exercise for the single most lucrative niche or industry you sell to. This should be the niche or industry that you love the most, are the most informed about, and have the most customers in.

The reason you'll be doing the most lucrative ones first is to support a "low-hanging fruit" VITO Blitz! Afterward you'll tackle the other niches or industries in your territory.

**Getting-to-VITO secret:**

VITO knows exactly how many customers he or she has, and what markets they sell to. You should, too. What would you say if VITO asked you, "How many customers do you have?" or "What percentage are in my market space?" Know the answer to these questions before you proceed to Getting-to-VITO step #3!

## GETTING-TO-VITO STEP #3: COLLECT YOUR HEADLINES

VITOs read Headlines. Headlines break preoccupation and are the genesis of your entire written, telephone, and/or in-person pitch to VITO. That's why you did the Value Inventory exercise in Step #2. This material is key to creating verbal Headlines and written correspondence for VITO.

### Do This

1. Grab your value inventory worksheet, go to Chapter 18, and create your "Elevator Pitch." If you run into any difficulty while trying to do this, (re)read Chapter 13, which begins on page 117.
2. Get yourself ready to pick up the telephone by doing a quick review of Chapter 19.

**Getting-to-VITO secret:**
VITOs get to the point and stay on point. They will only read and listen to what is of interest to them. For practice, I suggest you pick up the phone and call your own VITO and ask what he or she would say during a call to a *huge* prospect on your behalf. Listen to the words and phrases your VITO uses. Write them down. Don't memorize them; internalize them. You may want to tape-record their comments.

## GETTING-TO-VITO STEP #4: GET VITO NAMES AND NUMBERS

If you want to get to VITO, you'll need some VITO names! Pick a number from 1 to 100. My favorite is 57. Once you've got the number, purchase, beg, borrow, or abscond with a free trial of one or more of the 5,820,000 business directories that are currently available on the Internet. Now, cull from these lists VITO names. If you want, let's say, 57 VITOs, you'd best pick 30% more than that number due to "fallout" (VITOs do move about), list inaccuracy, and other problems that are inherent with business lists.

### *Do This*

1. Make sure, whatever list you select from, that the names comply with all of your parameters established in Step #1 (your TIP; see Appendix A).
2. Armed with your list, move on to Getting-to-VITO Step #5!

***Getting-to-VITO secret:***
The more VITOs you call, the faster you'll exceed your quota.

## GETTING-TO-VITO STEP #5: UNDERSTAND THE WAVE

If you want to get to VITO, you'll create a wave of correspondence that will precede your telephone call. Why not just pick up the phone and cold-call VITO? Well, you could do that. However, my experience shows that your hit rate will not be as high as it will be if you take just a little bit of time and create this correspondence wave that I've perfected over the years. So do it my way. And know that once you've got your wave created you'll be able to "repurpose" it time and time again adding just a few tailored elements.

### *Do This*

1. Flip to Chapters 13 and 14 and create a VITO correspondence.
2. Flip to Chapter 15, page 164, and create a VITO postcard.
3. Go to page 159 and create a VITO e-mail.
4. Plunge your browser into the online assets of Chapter 15 and take a look at my example of an e-presentation; then create one of your own.

5. Go back to your target list of VITO names and figure out which ones would be most likely to be predisposed to viewing an e-presentation. By the way, did you ask Tommie when you spoke to him or her if VITO would be predisposed to watching an e-presentation?

*Getting-to-VITO secret:*
Make every correspondence you write a quick read. No matter what sentence VITO (or anyone else) reads, it must quickly and concisely deliver something of relevance. Test your correspondence on any VITO you know. This can be your own VITO or one of your VITO prospects or customers.

### GETTING-TO-VITO STEP #6: PREPARE FOR TOMMIE

There is, in the final analysis, one person standing between you and VITO, and that's Tommie, VITO's private assistant. If you're going to send a wave of correspondence prior to picking up the phone and calling VITO, you'll need to do a little research. Get Tommie's name and build it into your wave. Prepare for the discussions you will have with Tommie. They're very important, and you can't skip them. Never forget: Tommie is God.

### *Do This*

1. Go to Chapter 19, pages 201–210, and read the role-plays between you and the gatekeeper receptionist and between you and Tommie.
2. Get your list of VITO names and telephone numbers ready, and hit the phone!

*Getting-to-VITO secret:*
Sound like a VITO, and treat Tommie like a VITO. If you do, you'll get along with Tommie very, very well.

### GETTING-TO-VITO STEP #7: LAUNCH THE WAVE

The wave of correspondence you're about to send will increase VITO's awareness, while at the same time piquing interest, building curiosity, and establishing credibility. The wave will create an environment in which your call will be an expected call. That will help you build greater confidence in getting to VITO.

### *Do This*

1. Quickly turn to Chapter 15, page 151, and select one of the five combinations of wave content that you feel will suit what you sell and the niche or industry you're selling to. Keep the following in mind:
   - Certain niches or industries respond better to certain types of correspondences.
   - Not every VITO will respond the same way to, let's say, e-mail. So don't try to shortcut the process and put all of your eggs in the easiest basket to create. There's power in diversity!
   - Be sensitive to the time of the month. It's been my experience that the second week of any month works the best for sending out your wave.
   - You'll find that if you send a wave once per month you'll have plenty of highly qualified VITO leads in your funnel.
2. Deploy your wave.

### *Getting-to-VITO secret:*

VITOs love positive results and the individuals who use intelligent processes to deliver them. When you show up after your creative wave of correspondence, you'll be showing VITO that you walk your talk. And that's not a bad idea.

### GETTING-TO-VITO STEP #8: PICK UP THE TELEPHONE

VITO is now sitting in his or her office looking at one or more pieces of correspondence that explains the importance of the call that you're about to make. One of several actions is about to take place when you, and no one else, pick up the phone and make the call to VITO at the appointed time.

1. VITO in person will pick up the phone and call you *prior* to your scheduled call. (I am not kidding: This *does happen,* and it *will happen* to you.)

2. Tommie will pick up the phone and call you *prior* to your scheduled call and give you the name of someone on VITO's list of trusted advisors or decision makers that they want you to contact.
3. Tommie will call you and tell you that VITO has no interest.
4. VITO will be waiting for your call.

### Do This

Be absolutely ready for each of these four situations.

*Situation One*

If VITO calls you *before* your scheduled call to them and says something close to "Got your stuff, tell me all about it," I strongly suggest you do the following:

- Don't tell VITO all about it!
- Simply ask VITO what he or she found interesting about your stuff. Or what he or she would like to do with the time you're spending together on the phone. Or what specifically he or she would like to discuss. *Don't* under any circumstances go into your product pitch mode!

*Situation Two*

If Tommie calls you and gives you the name of someone else at VITO, Inc. to call instead of VITO, I strongly suggest you do the following:

- Take the shunt.
- *Before* you hang up with Tommie, if you can, make every attempt to ask the following questions:
    1. Tommie, what can you tell me about Ms. Shunt's personality?
    2. Tommie, what types of challenges do you feel Ms. Shunt is facing?
    3. Tommie, what's Ms. Shunt's assistant's name?
    4. Tommie, do you think it's a good idea that I mention your name to Ms. Shunt?

- *After* you talk to Ms. Shunt:

   1. Determine whether there is a *real* opportunity for you to make a sale to VITO, Inc. In other words, was Ms. Shunt the right Decision Maker? Does she have the need, and does what you sell fit the need? If so, then move to the next step.

   2. Pick up the phone and leave a voice mail message for VITO or talk to VITO one on one and plant a thought (or leave a message) similar to the following: "Ms. Importanta, Tommie, your very thoughtful assistant, asked me to have a chat with Ms. Shunt, your [line of business executive], and I did just that. Ms. Shunt has a need for our services and has asked me [for additional information/to come out and see her/to put together a proposal/to make a presentation]. Ms. Importanta, before Ms. Shunt spends any more of her time and my organization incurs any additional expense we've got a question for you. Do you see any reason why you would not support an expenditure of somewhere between [$75,000 and $125,000] and become a customer of ours between now and the end of this [month]? To answer that question you can call me, Tony Parinello, right here at VITO Selling at 800-777-8486 between 3 and 6 p.m. Wednesday or Thursday of this week. Thanks for listening, and I look forward to your return call."

*Situation Three*

Tommie calls you and says that VITO has no interest. I strongly suggest you do the following:

- *Don't* say anything close to "thanks for letting me know."
- *Do* say something close to "Tommie, thanks for the call, and you know what? It doesn't surprise me in the least! Most of the [CEOs, presidents, and owners] that I approach have a similar response. It's hard to explain in one short page all of the ideas that we have for [process manufactures] here in [San Diego]. May I ask you to do me a personal favor?"

   1. Tommie says, "What's on your mind?" I suggest you ask, "Can you give me a general idea of what you and VITO are concerned about in the area of [two or three areas that you did not mention in your wave]?"

2. Tommie says, "I don't have time for this." I suggest you ask, "Is there anyone else that I might be able to chat with at VITO, Inc.?"

*Situation Four*

This is the situation where you call VITO directly. Before you pick up the phone, read Chapter 19. And begin living in sales heaven.

***Getting-to-VITO secret:***

VITOs get very few calls from salespeople. They will, however, talk to you if you are confident and determined and convinced that your message needs to be heard.

## GETTING-TO-VITO STEP #9: TALK TO TOMMIE

At some fateful point in time in your efforts in getting to VITO you will, I promise, find yourself on the phone with VITO's private assistant making your plea to have a touchpoint with VITO. You'll need to establish and maintain rapport with this all-important player.

### *Do This*

Treat Tommie like VITO. Go to Chapter 19 and read the how-to's of that simple tactic.

***Getting-to-VITO secret:***

Repeat: Treat Tommie like VITO. (You can never, ever get too much of a good thing.) Also, remember the gatekeeper (AKA Tommie) is GOD!

## GETTING-TO-VITO STEP #10: FOLLOW VITO'S LEAD

Believe it or not, VITOs begin the following-up, following-through process during their first interaction with anyone they sell to. Follow VITO's lead. Also, follow VITO's example.

### *Do This*

1. Pick your cause carefully: Not every opportunity is a profitable one. Remember, you don't need to sell everyone in your territory to be a "quota buster"—you only need to sell the right ones! Evaluate and calculate mutual value (see Chapters 3 and 4, pages 25–41).

2. Eliminate all loose ends as quickly as possible: Once you make any commitment to any VITO, make sure everything gets taken care of quickly. *Do everything you say you will do, no matter what.* If you neglect a (seemingly) minor issue, you will pay for it later on in the relationship.
3. Get in the habit of asking for what you want and need. VITO will deliver. VITO would not hesitate to ask you for a favor. Remember, you're an equal to VITO! And that includes asking for a referral (see Chapter 12).

**Getting-to-VITO secret:**
VITOs love people who do what they say they will do when they say they will do it. They love people like you!

## CONGRATULATIONS!

Whenever you can truthfully say that you have actually taken the time to do all ten steps outlined in this chapter, you may rest assured that you reside in the ranks of the top 5% of salespeople in America—the ones who pride themselves on finishing what they start!

Now that you're here, I invite you to stay in the ranks of the top achievers by embarking on a campaign of constant self-improvement. Take me up on the offers presented to you within the online assets sections of *Getting to VITO*.

If you would like to find out more about my live *Selling VITO* events, don't hesitate to call me at 1-800-777-VITO.

I look forward to hearing from you!

*Tony*

Anthony Parinello
800-777-VITO
www.gettingtovito.com

# Appendix A

---

# TEMPLATE OF IDEAL PROSPECTS

I've written about this process in each and every one of the five books on sales that I've written. Why? Because it's the way that I sell, it works, and I want to make sure that if you're a new reader of my work you don't miss out. If you've seen it before and you have not yet embraced this process as a part of your sales work, I'll ask you to reconsider for this one reason:

Today you've got less time than ever to sell, and you've also got larger quotas, more competition, more meetings to go to, more reports to write, and more pressure to get it all done. So why waste any time at all trying to sell to anyone who isn't predisposed to buy from you? Beats me.

Let's take a look.

Your Template of Ideal Prospects (TIP) sheet is an organized list of characteristics shared by your company's best customers. And if you take the time to complete and use what you're about to see, you'll never waste your time with deadbeat prospects again.

If you're saying, "I don't have any customers," "It's the beginning of a new year!" "I am a hunter!" "I just started this job!" "I just got a new territory," or whatever . . . worry not. The focus is on *your company's* best customers. Just about every company has a customer or two you can model this process with. My promise to you is this: If you take this step and live by this pre–sales call process you'll be getting to VITO in accounts that look just like your best customers. Which means they'll have similar needs, which means they'll respond favorably to your wave (see Chapter 15) and to your elevator pitch to VITO (see Chapter 18).

*Important note:*
When you reach for that list, make sure that it contains names of companies that are in the niche or industry that you've been tasked with selling to. (Yeah, I know . . . that's obvious!)

## LET'S GET IT DONE

Grab your current customer list (or your company's current customer list) and a notebook or perhaps a small personal tape recorder. You'll also need a pen or pencil and a large pad of paper. Put aside your laptop, Blackberry, PDA, and cell phone. You'll have no need for these "time savers." Not yet, anyway.

## GRAB THE KEYS TO YOUR CAR

No, you're not going out to make a sales call or take a friend to lunch. You're bound for the library—the biggest one in your area, one with a business research department worthy of the name.

If you're thinking, "What's wrong with the Internet?" I have one word for you: Everything. For starters, your competition is looking at the Internet. Let's just stop there, shall we? Trust me, the library is where you need to be. Once you're at the library, take a good, long look at that customer list you brought along. Then ask yourself the following question:

*What do my company's best current customers have in common?*

## A MOMENTOUS QUESTION

You know this . . . success leaves clues, a little trail of bread crumbs that when retraced will take you back to success—and so do your best customers. You'll be using all the library resources at your disposal to find answers to the key questions about your organization's existing customers. The first question is:

*What do my company's best current customers have in common?*

If the customer list you're holding in your hands is made up of more than one niche or industry, you'll need to break it down into subgroups. For example, if you're selling a product, service, or solution that's of interest to both retail and the automotive industry, you'll find that the specifics of each group's needs may be different and therefore should be taken into account. You'll also notice that different subgroups may have a limited number of commonalities . . . more bread crumbs. You'll be filling out a different TIP sheet for each of the niches or industries that you're wanting to sell to.

Look at that first question once again: "What do my company's best current customers have in common?" You may be tempted to answer by saying, "Hey, I know 'em when I see 'em" or some variation. Don't fall into that trap! The TIP will help you get very specific and focus like a laser beam, which will give you the power to cut through the B.S. out in your territory that eats up your precious selling time. Believe me, you owe your quota-busting career the fullest possible answer to that first question and the others that will soon follow.

Take a look at the blank TIP sheet that follows. Make several copies for your own use, or visit www.gettingtovito.com and click on Appendix A for copies you can print out. If you take the time to use the library's resources to develop detailed, meaningful first-draft answers to each of the sections of the TIP sheet, and if you then transfer your work into a duplicate of this form for a second draft, you will be well on your way to getting to VITO and bigger commission checks.

Read this TIP sheet carefully before you proceed any further!

# TEMPLATE OF IDEAL PROSPECTS

| Industry: | Category: |
|---|---|

### FILL IN ALL INFORMATION COMPLETELY.

| APPROVER | |
|---|---|
| DECISION MAKER(S) | |
| INFLUENCER(S) | |
| RECOMMENDOR(S) | |

### LIST 3 PROBLEMS YOU CAN SOLVE BY CATEGORY:

| APPROVER | 1.<br>2.<br>3. |
|---|---|
| DECISION MAKER | 1.<br>2.<br>3. |
| INFLUENCER | 1.<br>2.<br>3. |
| RECOMMENDOR | 1.<br>2.<br>3. |

### MY BEST CUSTOMERS IN THIS INDUSTRY HAVE:

| Between | and | [Salespeople] |
|---|---|---|
| Between | and | [Sales regions] |
| Between | and | [Annual Revenue] |
| Between | and | [Customers] |
| Between | and | [Channel Ptrs] |
| Between | and | [Quota increase] |
| Between | and | [Time to Sale] |

**OTHER CRITERIA:**

## WHAT DO WE HAVE HERE?

If you're remotely like me and hate research, consider yourself a better doer than planner, and don't think you have time for paperwork, spending at least a *full 8-hour day in the library* to develop your TIP sheet(s) will be a great investment in your career.

## WHAT IT LOOKS LIKE WHEN COMPLETE

Here is an example of my personal TIP sheet that has been completely filled out. Read it for reference and to get an idea of the kind of information you'll be tracking down. Don't assume that the answers that appear in this sample TIP sheet will have anything whatsoever to do with the answers that apply to your territory or your business!

# TEMPLATE OF IDEAL PROSPECTS

| **Industry:** Computer Manufacturers | **Category:** Industrial/Commerical |
|---|---|

## FILL IN ALL INFORMATION COMPLETELY.

| APPROVER | President, CEO, Owner |
|---|---|
| DECISION MAKER(S) | Vice President of Sales<br>Vice President of Marketing<br>Vice President of Channel Sales |
| INFLUENCER(S) | Director of Sales<br>Sales Manager<br>Head Sales Trainer |
| RECOMMENDOR(S) | Salespeople<br>Pre-Sales Technical Support<br>Inside Salespeople |

## LIST 3 PROBLEMS YOU CAN SOLVE BY CATEGORY:

| APPROVER | 1. Increase Shareholder value<br>2. Compress Time to Revenue<br>3. Increase high-margin, add on sales |
|---|---|
| DECISION MAKER | 1. Compress Time to Readiness<br>2. Over-achieve sales quota<br>3. Lower cost of sales and process time |
| INFLUENCER | 1. Reduce churn<br>2. Increase prospecting activity and results<br>3. Increase forecast accuracy |
| RECOMMENDOR | 1. Reduce prospecting reluctance<br>2. Eliminate rejection<br>3. Increase personal motivation |

## MY BEST CUSTOMERS IN THIS INDUSTRY HAVE:

| Between | 50 | and | 2,000 | [Salespeople] |
|---|---|---|---|---|
| Between | 5 | and | Unlimited | [Sales regions] |
| Between | 20,000,000 | and | Unlimited | [Annual Revenue] |
| Between | 100 | and | Unlimited | [Customers] |
| Between | 250 | and | Unlimited | [Channel Ptrs] |
| Between | 15% | and | 30% | [Quota increase] |
| Between | 2 months | and | 2 years | [Time to Sale] |

## OTHER CRITERIA:

Each of my customers are involved in a complex sale and have both "hunters" and "farmers" in the sales role and use some sort of outside sales training on a regular basis and also invest in conducting annual sales meetings.

## HERE'S THE WAY I USE MY TIP

That's my BEST customer. So, in evaluating any new prospect, I compare their characteristics to that list. *The more matches there are, the more predisposition the prospect will have to buy from me!* Personally, I will not call on anyone who isn't a perfect fit to my TIP. That's right: If I don't have a total match, I'll put that prospect on the back burner, and you know what? I've never had to go to the back-burner prospects yet, and I've been in this business for 18 years!

## BEFORE YOU LEAVE THE LIBRARY

After you complete your TIP sheet (or sheets: remember, you'll be completing one for each niche or industry you sell to), you'll need to get every single directory at the library and create a list all of the names of organizations in your territory that are a perfect match to your TIP(s). Or, if you prefer, you can purchase any number of lists from any number of sources. There are some sources (you'll see one of them at www.gettingtovito.com) that will match the list to your TIP!

Oh, before I forget. While you're at the library, take the time to check out a self-help book that you haven't read before!

# Appendix B

---

# MEET YOUR COACH

Hi. I'm Steve Dailey. I know, I know. You were innocently flipping through the book, and you came across this appendix at the end and wondered what the heck it was. Bumping into this may have been an afterthought for you.

But it may also be your first step on a winning trail.

As a matter of brief introduction, I'm a business coach. I've been coaching sales executives and sales professionals for over 20 years with the single goal of helping them attain what I call their Lifetime Best—LTB for short.

My philosophy is that labels like "top performer," "#1 in the sales contest," "120% over quota," and any other measurement you choose to name that compares what you do to the performance of others, or to the marketplace, or to what your boss thinks is a good performance . . . those labels really don't matter. What really counts is questions like these: Have you done your best compared to what *you* can do? Have you done better than any previous performance? Have you expanded, improved, accelerated, conquered the inertia that keeps you happy at performing at less than your true potential? *Have you achieved your LTB?*

Imagine what that level of performance would mean for you.

Would you like that? LTB performance every month, I mean? I'd like that for you . . . and, in fact, I will help you achieve that level of performance if you take to heart what you'll read about in this appendix.

Odds are, this is not the first sales book you have ever picked up. In fact, I'll bet you have read a bunch of sales books, probably gone to (or daydreamed through) some seminars on selling, read articles on selling, and maybe even listened to CDs on selling. You are in a continuous search for new ideas, insights, and techniques. You know that if you just found the right script, the right closing technique, the best way to find leads, you'd be at the top of your company and making a ton of dough. Right?

Reading, listening, attending are all a good start and great habits to maintain . . . but they just won't cut it when it comes to *really* winning in sales.

Why?

Because you will never get what you want when you

- Don't take *action* on what you know.
- Aim for the *wrong goal.*

Let me say it another way: *The keys to LTBs in selling* are

1. *Take action* on what you know.
2. Aim for the *right goal.*

Are you ready to roll up your sleeves and really kick some butt this time? Are you sort of sick of the mediocre level of performance you have been settling for? Great! Let's get to work.

## TAKE ACTION ON WHAT YOU KNOW

Throughout *Getting to VITO,* Tony did a terrific job of giving you a real-time update of his latest thinking and proven techniques on what really works in "selling high" in target companies and being effective with what you do when you get there.

But I've got a question for you: Did you *do* anything about it?

I'll wager it took you more than a day or two to get through this book. In the two days, two weeks, or two months it took you to expose your brain to Tony's system, did you *do the exercises? Write* anything down? *Practice* any of the stuff he suggested?

If you did, will you keep going? Will you keep learning from what you learned? Will you continue to practice until this stuff becomes part of you and your selling style? Have you done it enough that you could explain it to someone else?

You see, one of the things that all great sales professionals have in common is that they always want it fast. That's a good trait when it comes to market penetration, but when it comes to getting better at what they do, it's a handicap.

I've seen it a lot. A sales pro will read a book like *Getting to VITO* and *skim over the very exercises that will actually help him or her learn the stuff*. Or the person will do one or two exercises, get bored with it, and skip to the last chapter. Or—and this one is a killer—a salesperson will read the book, go through the exercises, *try the process once, and then give up because it didn't work!*

Let me coach you on this one. First, an assignment:

1. Do the exercises (fill in the blanks, create the value statements and headlines, write the letters, make the calls Tony mentions . . . all of it).
2. Practice the stuff for the next 90 days before you decide whether it works or not.

Now stop. After you read the assignment above, did you say or think anything like this?

> *I don't need that junk. I've been selling for X years; I don't need someone else telling me what to do. I've already tried most of that stuff, and some of it works and some of it doesn't. Blah, blah, weak excuse, blah, blah.*

If so, we just nailed the first thing that is keeping you from making the money you want, getting the most out of your selling career, and (probably) living in the house you really want or driving the car you want or paying for your kids' college like you want.

## YOU RESIST TAKING ACTION

If that's the case, it is because you are what I call *fat*. You are out of shape in the area of getting off your butt to try new things, and you know it—so you are going to come up with an excuse: You already know the stuff and you don't need to do anything about it. You know you are out of shape in taking action, and it's going to hurt to get back in shape.

I *know* you already know the stuff. But that's not the point! *Knowing* it and *doing* something about it are entirely two different things.

Taking *action* on the things you *already know* is the gateway to LTB.

And when I say "taking action" I'm not talking about trying it once or going through the motions. I mean really *taking action*. Taking action like a sprinter does when they come out of the starting blocks. Taking action like you intend to make your action count. Taking action like someone just lit your tail on fire.

But don't stop there.

*Take action* until you learn it. *Take action* until it becomes part of what you do. *Take action* until you can put your own personality into it and *own* it.

That's what I'm talking about. Take action on what you *already know*—and you'll be at the threshold of an LTB!

## AIM FOR THE RIGHT THING

If your current selling goal has anything to do with a quota, a company-defined sales number, or selling more stuff than someone else in your company or market—and if you use these targets to set your goals—then you're aiming at the wrong thing.

Look. As long as your life is inside of an umbrella called "Sales Career" or "Job," you'll never be happy and you will always underrealize your potential. Your sales career has to be *inside* of your life. Sales has to be one part of many parts of what you define as life. Life—and everything that comes with it—can't be a component or afterthought inside of your job.

When we make goals based on other people's standards, we make goals based on *someone else's* life.

Example: The boss sets a quota for you because he has an earning goal he has made in order to take care of *his* family and personal desires. Or perhaps your boss made the quota because someone else gave *him* a number to reach so that that person could take care of their financial portfolio so they can take care of their family needs and desires. It will eventually roll up to someone, somewhere who has their goals in proper alignment: life first, business second.

The only way for you to turn this around is to make sure you have personal goals, based on personal desires for *your* life and family, that *overwhelm* any goal that anyone else might set for you.

If you haven't ever done this, do it now: Get out a piece of paper and make three columns. At the top of the first column, put "My Life Goals." Write the following categories down this column, leaving three or four lines between each: Family, Fitness, Money, Career, Fun, and Personal. (Note: I've got an expanded category list that I use with most clients, but since you like it fast, this will at least get you down the right trail.)

Now, under each category write down two or three things you want to achieve in each area in the next three to five years. Be as specific as you can (for example, rather than "more money" put a specific amount of annual earnings). In the category "Personal" put goals for anything that doesn't fit in the other categories (like Spirituality, Community Service, Gifting, etc.).

At the top of the second column, write "Sales Equivalent." Next to each goal you wrote in the first column, write what you would have to achieve in annual sales performance to support that goal. If sales performance or dollars earned don't have anything to do with the goal (e.g., "get back into and maintain a size 6 dress" or "fit into my khakis with the 34-inch waist" under Fitness, or "go on a family ski trip every year" under Family) then determine what sort of annualized selling performance would buy the time to allow you to (for example) take more time exercising or take time off, guilt free, for a family trip.

At the top of the third column, write the name of your next sales period at the top (e.g., "November" or "Q4"). In this column, on the line adjacent to each "Sales Equivalent" that you wrote in the middle column, write what you would have to achieve in this period in your sales efforts that, when annualized, would total the number in the middle column.

It would look like this:

| My Life Goals | Sales Equivalent | November |
|---|---|---|
| Family | | |
| Fitness | | |
| Money | | |
| Career | | |
| Personal | | |

Now I know this is a down-and-dirty course in goal setting—but here's the bottom line: What you have just done is ordered your priorities in such a way that you *own* your sales career rather than allowing it to own you. Further, *you* have set your goals, not someone else.

You might be asking, "What if my goals for the month total up less than my quota?" Hmm . . . are you telling me that your boss or company wants more for your family, lifestyle, and future than you do? I'd say, adjust your goals upward, because more is obviously available to you.

Or maybe you're asking, "What if my goals are way beyond what I have ever achieved?" I say, "Great!" and go back to LTB principle #1: Take action on what you know. Time's a-wastin'!

When you have clear goals that are defined by what is important to you, *personally,* you will maximize your current efforts and eventually find yourself in a selling or business environment that will satisfy what you are working to achieve. But as long as your goals are based on what someone else thinks you should do, you will be stuck underperforming against your potential and allowing your sales career to *be* your life instead of *part* of your life.

Again, the LTB principle: *Aim at the right things—and the right things are yours to decide.*

## A POSTSCRIPT

You can't do it alone. I know you have a lot of self-confidence and you know what you're doing and you've done it for years and you don't need any help and all that blah, blah. I've heard resistance to support more times and in more ways than you have heard prospects' excuses for not buying your products.

So let's get past all of that and tell the truth. When was the last time you accomplished anything you are proud of without support, encouragement, guidance, and/or coaching from a committed partner?

Be honest. The answer is "Never."

Face it. You will *never* take action and stay with something new until it becomes part of you without knowing that someone is watching. And you will *never* aim at the right things and keep a long-term perspective in view without someone reminding you of what you said was most important.

You need a coach. If you really want LTB, you need the support, collaboration, and guidance of someone that is an expert in navigating new achievement trails. You need the "juice" that comes from having someone shoulder to shoulder in your process of achieving new success and a partner in making sure every day, week, and month counts on the road to achieving the things that are truly important in life.

Find a coach of your own. Call Tony. Or call me. I'll either help you personally or help you find someone that will help to light up your future.

Remember: It's not about the stuff in the book—it's about taking action on the stuff in the book. And it's not about their goals, it's about your goals.

You can reach me by email at sdailey@primefocuscoaching.com, or visit www.primefocuscoaching.com.

You can reach Tony Parinello by calling 1-800-777-VITO.

Great success to you and my sincere wish for your LTB!

# Appendix C

# THE GREATEST TIMESAVING TOOL IN THE FREE WORLD

If you have plowed your way through this book and gotten to this point, you know that I am not a technology whiz. I do, however, totally subscribe to automating any- and everything that will save me time. Remember, I am a salesperson and I like taking shortcuts!

For a good many years I kept track of prospect names, telephone numbers, addresses, e-mails, and tons of other information using a host of different systems like Post-It notes, bar napkins, Rolodex systems, journals, databases, sales force automation (SFA) tools, desktops, laptops, PDAs, Blackberrys, and customer relationship management (CRM) systems. Truth be told, they all had the same problem.

Me.

It was (but no longer is) as they say: "garbage in, garbage out." So, in the past five years, I made a conscious decision to pay closer attention to what I was "inputting" and what I was "inputting" my information into. During that time, I've migrated along the technology highway, and today I am proud to say that I use the latest web-based CRM on demand system that Internet whiz kids have to offer. With the new VITO selling process that we've been talking about for the past 60,000 words or so, it becomes critically important to keep track of the who, the what, and the when of our sales actions with VITO.

## TEN BITS AND BYTES

By my count there are ten different critical bits of information that must be monitored and tracked in getting to VITO. It's been my personal experience that if you forget any of them your lack of attention to detail will come back and bite you right where you don't want to be bitten at a time when being bitten is not going to be much fun.

### *Critical Bit of Information Number One*

You'll remember that there are five different and important categories or positions at VITO, Inc. They are board members (or board of advisors), the Approver, the Decision Maker(s), the Influencer(s), and the Recommender(s). It will serve you well to keep each and every name of these all-important players at the ready whenever you are talking to anyone at VITO, Inc.—which certainly includes VITO!

*My advice:* Make sure your CRM system can keep track each player mentioned. Find a note field or create a database that includes the following information:

| Position | Name | Title | Company | Date last contacted |
|---|---|---|---|---|
| Board Member #1 | | | | |
| Board Member #2 | | | | |
| Board Member #3 | | | | |
| Board Member #4 | | | | |
| Board Member #5 | | | | |
| VITO | | | | |
| Tommie | | | | |
| Decision Maker(s) | | | | |
| Influencer(s) | | | | |
| Recommender(s) | | | | |

### *Critical Bit of Information Number Two*

What's currently on VITO, Inc.'s plate? What are the goals, plans, and objectives of each player, and when do they need to be accomplished?

*My advice:* Keep it simple and straightforward so you can read it quickly *before* each interaction with anyone at VITO, Inc. (The key word in that sentence is *before.*) My guess is that if it's too long you won't take the time to write it, or read it! Allow yourself just 10 words or so for each player. Take a look at this example:

| Position | Name | Critical objectives |
|---|---|---|
| VITO | Ms. Importanta | Capture Pacific Rim market by 10/1 |
| | | Contain expenses by 11/1 |
| | | Increase shareholder distributions by 12/1 |
| Tommie | Jackie McCall | Provide infrastructure support to team |
| Decision Maker | Joe Kickass | Build all collateral for launch by 8/1 |
| | | Increase reporting accuracy by 50% before 11/1 |
| Influencer | Seemore Knoitall | Create RFQ, make no mistakes. No time frame |
| Recommender | Jimmy Last | Get the job done, have more time off |

### *Critical Bit of Information Number Three*

What's your Value Proposition for VITO, Inc.? If there is one critically important fact about getting to VITO, it's this: how and when you can deliver value to VITO, Inc.

*My advice:* Make sure that you have a place in your CRM system to articulate value in each of the following categories:

| Name | Category | Value statement |
|---|---|---|
| Ms. Importanta | Hard value | Increase revenue by as much as 11% in 6 months |
| | | Contain nonvalue expense up to 7% in 1 month |
| | Soft value | Increase brand awareness |
| | | Increase customer service perception |
| | Minimum acceptable value | Impact shareholder value by 2 points |
| | Time-to-value | No later than Q3 |
| | Lifetime value | Over $3,000,000 in 5 years |

### Critical Bit of Information Number Four

VITO correspondence is key to your getting to VITO, and Headlines are key for your correspondence to be successful. Which headline did you use? What wave did you select, and what correspondence modalities did you choose to use? First-class letter, postcard, e-presentation, fax, or some combination of these attention-getting pieces of correspondence?

*My advice:* Your CRM system must keep track of what you sent, what headline you pitched, and when your call will be made to VITO. I strongly suggest that it look something like this:

| VITO | Headline | Wave | Call on/at |
|---|---|---|---|
| Mr. Benefito | Increase shareholder value, Invest $500,000, and receive a 2,000% return in 6 months | #2 | 5/14 9:00 |

*Important note:* Categorize your wave by assigning it a number. I invite you to use the system I spoke about in Chapter 15, "Wave Goodbye to Seemore."

### Critical Bit of Information Number Five

At a moment's notice you've got to be ready to give your elevator pitch or telephone/in-person opening statement monologue to VITO. Could you bat it out right now . . . without giving it a second thought? Once you deploy your wave you must be ready to articulate your value to VITO. (Remember, VITO could beat you to the punch and call you!) We've spent a good deal of time on this topic, so it stands to reason that our CRM system must provide an instant preview of the hook portion of what we're going to say when VITO picks up the phone!

*My advice:* Your CRM system must at a bare minimum provide the date and time you'll be calling VITO (see Critical Bit of Information Number Four) and a short narrative of the essence of what you should be saying.

| *VITO* | *Call on/at* | *Headline* | *Your hook* |
|---|---|---|---|
| Mr. Benefito | 5/14 9:00 | Increase shareholder value Invest $500,000, and receive a 2,000% return in 6months | One of our ideas generated a 2,000 percent return in 6 months for another CEO in your industry |

*Important note:* The hook, as you'll recall, is not your entire elevator pitch; review Chapters 17 and 18 for more information.

### Critical Bit of Information Number Six

If VITO isn't in, you'll be leaving a voice mail message. You'll recall that leaving just one message most likely won't generate enough interest to prompt VITO to return your call. You'll need several voice mail messages, and you'll need to leave one each week for no less than seven weeks. If you're as quick with math as I am, you're saying "Tony, that's seven messages!" That's exactly why you'll need the help of your CRM system and your word processor to keep track of them.

*My advice:* Create a word processing file that stores the script for all seven of your voice mail messages, and number them (one through seven). Your CRM system can look something like this:

| VITO | Call on/at | Elevator pitch | Left V/M | Number |
|------|-----------|----------------|----------|--------|
| Mr. Benefito | 5/14 9:00 | Increase shareholder value Invest $500,000, and receive a 2,000% return in 6 months | 5/14 | 1 |
| | 5/21 | | 5/21 | 2 |
| | 5/28 | | 5/28 | 3 |

*Important note:* Make sure that you store your voice mail scripts in a safe place that is easily accessible and backed up regularly and that your script allows for tailoring your message for each of the many VITOs you'll be calling.

### Critical Bit of Information Number Seven

At some point during your interaction with VITO you'll most likely be shunted to someone within VITO's rank and file. When this happens, you'll need to leave a trail of bread crumbs so you can re-create your pathway to your sale. Why? Because, that piece of information will serve you well in your quest to shorten your sales cycle and streamline your sales process. Let's call this your "Shunt" file.

*My advice:* Who you get shunted to is as important as who did the shunting! Make sure your CRM system keeps track of the "to and by" of each shunt:

| VITO | Headline | Wave | Call on/at | Shunt to/by |
|------|----------|------|-----------|-------------|
| Mr. Benefito | Increase share-holder value Invest $500,000, and receive a 2,000% return in 6 months | #2 | 5/14 9:00 | Joe Kickass/ Tommie |

### Critical Bit of Information Number Eight

What did you find out when you talked to VITO, Tommie, or the person you were shunted to? What critical bits of information did they impart to you? You'll need a place on your CRM system to summarize what you found out . . . but keep it short! Remember, if it's too long you won't want to write it or read it!

*My advice:* A quick notes field will work just fine.

| Wave | Call on/at | Shunt to/by | Critical information |
|------|-----------|-------------|----------------------|
| #2 | 5/14 9:00 | Joe Kickass/ Tommie | Needs quick turnaround and delivery on knowledge-based tool and web-based CRM . . . decision by 7/1 |

### Critical Bit of Information Number Nine

In real estate sales it's often said that "location, location, location" will make the sale. When it comes to getting to VITO and making the sale, I'll put my money on "follow-up, follow-up, follow-up." This is the quickest way to build trust and credibility and show VITO that you are a salesperson of the utmost integrity.

*My advice:* Don't go it alone . . . don't leave it to your memory! (Or any form of handwritten note taking.) Use your CRM system to assist in this all-important date-dependent task. Your CRM system will remind you of what you promised and when you promised it by.

| Shunt to/by | Critical information | Follow up/by |
|---|---|---|
| Joe Kickass/ | Needs quick turnaround/ | e-presentation/ |
| Tommie | delivery on knowledge-based | 6/1 |
| | tool . . . decision by 7/1 | |

*Important note:* Simple, isn't it? Don't forget to set an alarm on your CRM in plenty of time to create the e-presentation and get it to Joe Kickass by 6/1!

### Critical Bit of Information Number Ten

Let's get personal! What do you know about VITO and the critical players at VITO, Inc.? There are three dates in particular that I invite you to know and use to build all-important rapport.

Date Number One:    VITO's birthday
Date Number Two:    VITO's anniversary with the company
Date Number Three: VITO's wedding anniversary

*Important note number one:* I'll put emphasis on knowing these dates for VITO, Tommie, and the person(s) whom you'll get shunted to.

*Important note number two:* Of course you'll be sending a specialty card for all of the three dates. *Remember,* when you send the card for VITO's wedding anniversary, send it a few days early so it can serve as a silent reminder of that date . . . just in case it slipped VITO's mind.

### Bonus Critical Bit of Information Number Eleven!

Yeah, I know I said there were only 10, but what about VITO-to-VITO referrals? You'd best keep track of whom VITO has referred you to. Because you know they're going to ask: "Tony, did you ever wind up doing business with Mr. Big?" At that point you don't want to be caught off guard, so . . . your CRM system should look something pretty darned close to this:

| Referred to/by | Critical information | Follow up by |
|---|---|---|
| Mr. Big/<br>  Ms. Importanta | Mr. Big had no immediate needs | 12/1 |

## SUMMARY

Sure, all of this is a lot of information to keep track of, but you know what? You don't have to keep track of it at all! That's the job of your CRM system. Consider the time it takes for you to input it as an investment, money in the bank, so to speak. I hope you won't opt out and decide to perform this all-important task manually. Go to www.gettingtovito.com for additional information on CRM systems that will take the grunt work out of getting to VITO!

# INDEX